What Mama Never Told You About the Afterlife . . .

Conversations about Faith, Salvation, & Universalism

By

Terry L. Craig

What Mama Never Told You About the Afterlife,
Conversations About Faith, Salvation, & Universalism

Published by Wild Flower Press, Inc.
P.O. Box 2532
Leland, NC 28451
Website: www.wildflowerpress.biz

This book or parts thereof may not be reproduced or altered in any form, stored in a retrieval system, or transmitted in any form by any means—electronic, digital, mechanical, photocopy, recording, or otherwise—without prior written permission of the publisher, except as provided by United States of America copyright law.

Copyright © 2012 by Terry L. Craig.

All rights reserved

The photo on the front cover was taken by Bill Craig. (© 2014 Bill Craig)

Every effort was made to accurately depict the Internet works of those who were referenced in this book with the locations of their remarks noted in the footnotes and the dates they were accessed. However, keep in mind that on the Internet, content that is there today can be changed or removed tomorrow. Any inaccuracies on our part are unintentional.

ISBN 13: 978-0-9909616-5-9

Unless otherwise noted, all Scripture quotations in this book are taken from the HOLY BIBLE, NEW INTERNATIONAL VERSION® (NIV). Copyright © 1973, 1978, 1984 International Bible Society. Used by permission of Zondervan. All rights reserved.

Scriptures marked NLT are taken from the Holy Bible, New Living Translation®, Copyright 1996. Used by permission of Tyndale House Publishers, Inc., Wheaton, Illinois 60189. All rights reserved.

Scripture quotations marked AMP are taken from the Amplified Bible® Copyright © 1954, 1958, 1962, 1964, 1965, 1987 by The Lockman Foundation. Used by permission." (www.Lockman.org)

Scripture quotations marked NASB are taken from the New American Standard Bible®, Copyright © 1960, 1962, 1963, 1968, 1971, 1972, 1973, 1975, 1977, 1995 by The Lockman Foundation. Used by permission." (www.Lockman.org)

Scripture quotations marked MSG are taken from The Message. Copyright © 1993, 1994, 1995, 1996, 2000, 2001, 2002. Used by permission of NavPress Publishing Group.

Scripture quotations marked KJV are taken from the King James Version of the Bible which is Public Domain.

Scripture quotations marked YLT are taken from Young's Literal Translation Bible which is Public Domain.

Printed in the United States of America

Dedication

To my Lord

To my father, Lou Seyler

And to Bill

Acknowledgements:

I want to express my gratitude to so many people who have encouraged and inspired me to seek God first—among them my precious sister, Jo Ann, and Melody Horn who led me to His door.

Thanks to my pilot husband, Bill, who has taken *thousands* of pictures of the sky. One of his photos graces the cover of this book. (And yes, this is an actual photo, taken over central Florida.)

I give thanks to Sarah Arnold and Kim Craig who assisted in editing the first drafts of this book.

Thanks also to Matthew Raley, for graciously allowing me to share much of his article, *God's Redemptive Justice*, from his site, Tritone Life (http://tritonelife.com).

Let me express gratitude to the many people who have upset me, rattled my thinking, challenged my views, and sometimes really made me angry in conversations about faith. :-) Without you, perhaps people like me would never truly search our hearts or press in for more of the Lord.

I want to apologize for sometimes not expressing myself with God's Love. I think all people need and deserve truth, but I see now that there have been times, in my haste to express myself or in the heat of the moment, frustration and sarcasm have outed their presence in my heart.

Let us all remember the saying: *Love without truth deceives. Truth without love destroys.*

TABLE OF CONTENTS

- 6   Special Notes about Scripture Quotes and Footnotes
- 7   "WHAT IF?"—Is God offended by honest questions?
- 9   A glossary of terms
- 11   **CHAPTER 1—Let's Not Ignore the Gorilla in the Room**
- 17   **CHAPTER 2—The Call of Intergalactic Rabbit Trails**
- 21   **CHAPTER 3—Why *did* Jesus come to Earth? Beginning at the Beginning**
- 24   **CHAPTER 4—Introduction to a Mystery! The debate over meaning**
- 26   **CHAPTER 5—Death, Heaven, Hell, and the Resurrection**
  - 26 What is Death?
  - 27 Who is in Heaven Now?
  - 28 Picturing Heaven
  - 30 Picturing Hell
  - 36 Capitalizing on Common Misunderstandings about Hell and Death
  - 36 The 3 Elements of the UR Equation
  - 37 A Brief List of Scriptures that Speak of the Resurrection
- 46   **CHAPTER 6—When Are Words . . . Just Words?**
  - 46 Must we always take Scripture at face value?
  - 48 The words of Gerry Beauchemin
  - 54 Will Jesus "drag" all people into heaven?
  - 56 Jesus' *Actions* Speak as Loud as His Words
  - 58 Does the Bible speak of the salvation/reconciliation of "all sentient beings"?
- 64   **CHAPTER 7—Lost in Translation?**
  - 64 *Is it FOREVER or TEMPORARY?*
  - 65 God's Redemptive Justice
  - 65 How a "limited time" (a.k.a. "proportional" Hell) argument further loses merit
  - 66 CONTEXT—Why Forever Isn't Temporary
  - 69 PROPORTIONALITY: The idea that "Degrees" of sin equals degrees of punishment
  - 70 Is God limited by our CONCEPT?
  - 70 Is reality somehow limited by LANGUAGE?
  - 72 What IS a METAPHOR anyway?
- 75   **CHAPTER 8—What IS the "Faith that Saves" People?**
  - 76 Faith in what or whom? Is it that all faiths are one or that there is only one faith?
  - 76 Do/Can Demons Have "Faith" That Saves?
  - 77 The Gospel
  - 77 Can/Does the Gospel "Evolve"?
  - 79 Can Someone Get Saved on Their Deathbed?
  - 79 Can Someone Be Saved and Not Know It?
  - 80 Can People Be Reconciled to God After Death?
  - 81 The Bible says that ALL people will be "resurrected" but what does that mean?
  - 82 The Two Groups of People Who are Resurrected in The New Testament
  - 83 The Importance of Sharing the Gospel of Jesus Christ During this Lifetime
  - 84 Today Is the Day That Counts
  - 84 A Quote from Mother Theresa

CHAPTER 8 (continued)

- 85 New Testament examples of God's love for people and His desire to set them free
- 86 Boundaries? In the "Age of Grace" We Don't Need No Stinkin' Boundaries! *Or do we*?
- 87 What IF . . . ?
- 88 Are we "keepin' it real" or just makin' it weird?
- 89 The World's Infatuation with the Walking Dead
- 91 A List of New Testament Scriptures that Connect Salvation to Personal Faith in Christ

94   CHAPTER 9—THE PARABLES

98   CHAPTER 10—The BIG picture

104   CHAPTER 11—Christian history and concepts of the past
- 104 *Apokatastasis*

106   CHAPTER 12—Scriptures on Topics other than Hell that Don't Work with Universalism
- 106 Who is Your Daddy?
- 108 The Holy Spirit
- 111 The Church is the Body of Christ
- 112 Light and Darkness
- 112 Intercession—Love Stepping into Our Timeline
- 112 Spiritual Warfare and Deliverance
- 113 The Power of Personal Faith in Jesus
- 113 Darkness Can't Fight Darkness and Have the Final Victory
- 114 "Overcomers" and Those Who are "Victorious"
- 115 Ambassadors
- 115 Justice
- 117 What Was it About The Pharisees that Grieved and Angered Jesus?

119   CHAPTER 13—Revelations that Changed the Course of Christendom

121   CHAPTER 14—Truth and Love . . . Are They the Romeo and Juliet of the Bible?

124   CHAPTER 15—Making Christianity about Jesus Christ

130   Other Books from Wild Flower Press, Inc.

132   Wild Flower Press, Inc. Upcoming Books plus Articles and Bible Studies

Special Notes About Scripture Quotes and Footnotes

I realize that the eyes of most people will glaze over after reading several verses of Scripture. *Mindful of this fact,* I have listed many of the issues/questions/answers in the *Table of Contents.* You can jump to the topics that interest you the most and get to the meat of them right away. Please know that there is *so much more* to see and ponder than will be written here, but I want to inspire the courage in others to think for themselves and give them some footing, in the hope each will continue to seek God and honestly search the Scriptures.

Please note that **with the exception** of text taken from the Amplified Bible® everywhere that you see comments in brackets [ ] before, after, or within a scripture quote, these are comments added by me for clarity. An example of my own clarification would be:

> **John 12:32** [Jesus speaking] "And I, when I am lifted up from the earth, will draw all people to myself."

In ALL cases where you see an underline, words in *italics*, or text in **bold** within a scripture quote, these were added by me for emphasis.

Please note that passages in the Amplified Bible® often contain words in brackets [ ] and parentheses ( ) and these are in the actual text of this version of Scripture—so the comments in parentheses and brackets in these quotes are *theirs*, not mine. This is done by the translators of this version to enhance the reader's understanding, to give a clearer idea of the nuances in Old Testament Hebrew or New Testament Greek. Everywhere that I use a quote from this version of the Bible, it will be noted at the end of the quote like this "—AB" or "—Amplified Bible An example:

> **1 Peter 3:15** "But in your hearts set Christ apart as holy [and acknowledge Him] as Lord. Always be ready to give a logical defense to anyone who asks you to account for the hope that is in you, but do it courteously and respectfully." —AB

Without any apologies, the meditations offered in this book will be based on Scripture.

* * *

"WHAT IF . . . ?"

You know, I don't think God has a problem with questions. He's not wringing His hands at the thought we might ask a question He can't answer. And I don't think He's ever offended by an honest question. I believe I can talk to Him about *any*thing. Seriously. Of course, that doesn't obligate Him to do what I want, or zip me an immediate answer, or give me a comprehensive response—but if I have a question regarding my walk with Him, I believe He has both the desire and the means to answer me. See, that's one of the *wonderful* things about God. He's not dead! He's not just a book or a set of laws—He's *alive* and able to handle any question or problem I might have. What He waits for is my heart to be open to what He has to say. If I fix my mind and heart onto the answer I want or what I think He *must* say or do, I may not hear His answer.

Aware of the grace He has shown to me, I try not to be put off by the honest questions other people have. What DOES concern me is when people go from honest questions or considering possibilities to an idea that "*has* to be true" or saying what God *must* do in order to retain His godhood . . . simply because they've decided it's "fair" or "good." Which brings us to the topics of Heaven and Hell and the fodder for conversations that I want to share with you. . . .

So who am I? Am I a scholar or a leader or a teacher? Nope. I am an ordinary person who loves the Lord, loves to encourage people to trust God for answers—loves to see the looks on their faces when *their* God-given logic kicks in and they allow their minds to become engaged with what the Bible says to us. That's the whole point. If more Christians sought God, read the Bible, and discussed what it actually says, we wouldn't get in so many stews over revelations that people claim to have.

While some Christian leaders call Universal Reconciliation or Universalism heresy, others are calling it a way of seeing the Gospel of Jesus as "all inclusive"—and in our politically correct world, the word "inclusive" has a lot of traction. But few people seem to know exactly what the beliefs of Universalism (a.k.a. Universal Reconciliation, or Universal Restoration) actually entail. You might ask, "*Who cares?*" If you are a Christian, <u>you</u> should. The methods that BOTH Traditional Christians and Universalists use to come to their conclusions will have a lasting impact on how those around us see God, Scripture, and history.

Those who know me know that, while I have a generally friendly nature, I like to get to the bottom line and speak openly—but given the passionate nature of the debate over this topic and the fact that people reading this will only be seeing text on a page (rather than hearing all that is in my heart) I will make efforts to convey my ideas with respect. Sometimes, I may not have found a soft way to state what I see as a fact or to pose a question, but please don't read anything here thinking that my intent was to verbally slap someone.

This book isn't an argument; it's an invitation to ask honest questions and really chew on the ideas that people present to us. I hope that one or more of the things presented here will help people to pursue and apprehend more of what <u>Jesus</u> has in mind when He speaks of faith, salvation, love, and discipleship—what it means to *know* Him and journey with Him. The thoughts and questions I present here aren't just in reference to Universalism but to a gathering storm of opinions that will increasingly be brought to every Christian's doorstep, to our schools, churches, and places of work.

Hebrews 2:1 So we must listen very carefully to the truth we have heard, or we may drift away from it.—NLT

If you believe in "Christian" Universalism (or Universal Reconciliation, or Universal Restoration, or simply UR) and after reading this you feel I have misunderstood the elements of this belief, or neglected a key piece of information, feel free to send comments through the contact link on the Wild Flower Press, Inc. website (www.wildflowerpress.biz). If I believe your idea merits consideration, I'll update future versions of the book—but I reserve my right to voice a rebuttal as well. :-) If you have a sincere question, feel free to contact me through the above link as well.

I hope to set before you what I understand to be some of the basic elements of Universalism and UR, and some of what can be seen in the Bible about salvation and the Christian life.

So go ahead and ask your "what if" questions, be willing to entertain MY "what if" questions—then be willing to let <u>God</u> make the pathway straight. Be open to hear Him speak and then to express yourself wisely and in love.

In Him,

Terry Craig

PS

I'm a person who writes notes in a lot of the books I buy. I'm hoping that many of you will study what is written here and make YOUR OWN notes throughout the pages. I've even included a few blank pages at the end for your own Endnotes. :-)

A glossary of terms

. . . that will help the rest of the book make sense

Universalism

It is a term that encompasses a WIDE range of beliefs, and, as I understand it, can be anything from the belief that "all paths lead to God or 'the divine," to "a theological doctrine that all human beings will eventually be saved . . ." [i]

In this book, however, we will only address the form of Universalism that teaches that all the people who ever existed will eventually be saved by Jesus Christ.

"Christian Universalism"

This is the view that, because of the cross of Jesus, *everyone* will be saved regardless of what they believe or do here in this life. According to the Christian Universalism Association website: "All people are God's children and no one will be left behind." [ii] Whether or not others accept this group's ideas as "Christian," it is a title they have given themselves.

Universal Reconciliation or Universal Restoration (abbreviated UR)

Those who believe in Christian Universalism (as defined above) and UR have expanded what they believe is a narrow view of salvation (as traditional Protestant and Evangelical Christians would see it) and they focus their ministry on what they often refer to as "inclusiveness"—which means they believe *everyone* has a desirable outcome (is saved, reconciled to God). [iii] NONE of these beliefs is new, but they are seeing a surge of popularity in seeker-sensitive and relativistic settings. The teachings of these movements promote the belief that *all* beings (all people, demons, and even Satan himself) will *eventually* be reconciled to God. In addition, those who believe in UR state that, even after a person's physical death, there will be ways to repent and be welcomed into Heaven until everyone is "reconciled to God." Because they teach that *Jesus Christ* is the means by which all beings are reconciled, they consider their ideas "Christian" in nature.

Again, there *are* groups of "Universalists" who *don't* see Jesus Christ as necessary in their belief system (they may think of Jesus in some "teacher of spiritual truths" kind of way, but don't see His atonement as essential). The religious views of this kind of "Universalist" aren't addressed in this book, since they stake no claims upon Christianity.

If you are a "Christian Universalist" (a.k.a. one who believes in Universal Reconciliation or Universal Restoration) and it bothers you that I have simply chosen the word "Universalist" or "UR" to refer to your beliefs throughout this book—I apologize but the long titles are ungainly when one has to use them over and over. I hope the clarification here will suffice.

---

[i] "universalism" *Merriam-Webster.com*. 2011. http://www.merriam-webster.com (13 October 2011).

[ii] from the index page of The Christian Universalist Association http://www.christianuniversalist.org/ (13 October 2011)

[iii] There are a few forms of Universalism in which the people believe the worst-case scenario after death is a neutral outcome where a person simply ceases to exist after death (this being referred to as "annihilation") similar to what Jehovah's Witnesses believe. We won't take the time to address this idea in the book.

Christianity

There are so many people with so many views who would call themselves "Christian" that I also feel the need to define Christianity as it will be presented in this book. Wikipedia has what I consider a good overall description of how the word "Christian" came about, so I will include it here:

> The Greek word *christianos*—meaning "follower of Christ"—comes from *christos*—meaning "anointed one"—with an adjectival ending borrowed from Latin to denote adhering to, or even belonging to, as in slave ownership. In the Greek Septuagint, *christos* was used to translate the Hebrew *Mašíaḥ,* (messiah), meaning "[one who is] anointed." In other European languages, equivalent words to 'Christian' are likewise derived from the Greek, such as 'Chrétien' in French and 'Cristiano' in Spanish.
>
> The first recorded use of the term (or its equivalent in other languages) is in the New Testament, in Acts 11:26, which states ". . . in Antioch the disciples were first called Christians." The second mention of the term follows in Acts 26:28, where Herod Agrippa II replies to Paul the Apostle, "Do you think that in such a short time you can persuade me to be a Christian?" The third and final New Testament reference to the term is in 1 Peter 4:16, which exhorts believers, ". . . if you suffer as a Christian, do not be ashamed, but praise God that you bear that name." [iv]

For the purposes of this book, when I refer to an individual as a "Christian" (not as part of an organizational title they have given themselves), I am directly connecting the word "Christian" to someone who has *believed* the gospel of Jesus Christ. The same applies when I refer to "a believer," "a brother," "a sister," or someone who is "in Christ." The following is a simple form of the gospel of Jesus Christ:

> Jesus is the only begotten Son of God; He IS God, equal in substance, power, and nature to Father God. He left the glories of Heaven, was born a flesh and blood human being, lived a sinless life here on earth, and died on a cross in *our* place, for *our* sins, as a ransom for *our* souls—for *none* of us can free ourselves. Jesus was buried, and after three days and nights, He rose from the grave in an eternal, glorified body, and is now at the right hand of the Father in heaven. His kingdom will have no end.

Further, I believe the *offer* of salvation through faith is open to *all* people, but each person, once they are of sufficient maturity to be accountable for their decisions, must choose to accept God's offer while they live on earth (inhabit flesh).

There are more things that Christians believe and do that define finer points of doctrine or denominations, but simply put, if we *believe* the gospel of Jesus Christ and confess it, we are saved (Romans 10:9-10). **If** we have truly done this (let Jesus Christ become our sole source of righteousness and Life), our lives will increasingly attest to the fact that we are followers (disciples) of Jesus Christ. *Evidence* that you are saved is a growing love of others, and the fruit of the Holy Spirit in your life. The source of our transformation is the Holy Spirit (the Spirit of Jesus Christ) who comes to live IN us. Jesus is the hope of glory.

[iv] http://en.wikipedia.org/wiki/Christian (February 24, 2012)

CHAPTER 1—Let's not ignore the Gorilla in the room

When it happened, there was a big public blow up over remarks made by mega pastor Rob Bell who openly questioned some of the traditional doctrines on Hell. Several issues came into public awareness and continue to simmer concerning whether or not there is a Hell, whether it is temporary or forever, and whether or not it is fair to use the topic of Hell to win converts.

This is a conversation the church should welcome. We would be wise to discuss what salvation IS, our methods for determining truth, and our means of sharing what we believe with others.

Should Christian evangelism revolve around the existence of Hell? *No!*

I cringe when I hear some preacher going on and *on* about Hell in an effort to scare people into Heaven or make them think of a salvation prayer as "fire insurance."

The Christian life (and all that flows from it) should be rooted in and centered upon Jesus Christ, *not* upon systems . . . or the avoidance of Hell. Acceptance of Jesus as the Lord and King of your life should be just the *beginning* of a love relationship that will continue into eternity!

To attempt to lead people to take Jesus as their Savior merely to escape Hell is like an old fashioned shot-gun wedding (where one party was forced to marry the other at gunpoint). Could such a marriage be happy for either party? Jesus, the King of Glory, my savior, my brother, my friend, shouldn't be presented as the lesser of unpleasant outcomes OR as some default option. Jesus came so that we might have abundant Life, both here AND in what comes next. Jesus came so that we could have a relationship with the Father starting *now*. Jesus came to set us free to love, starting *now*.

Some church leaders fly at the "heresy" of the Universalists' challenge to traditional views about Hell—but BOTH sides are often ignoring the more salient issues while they engage in an a circular argument that neither side can settle. Neither side seems to be helping the rest of us to see what *should* be the central issues of the debate.

FOR THE RECORD, although I personally believe that God will judge all people (and yes, punish some of them for their deeds here on earth), I want to say that I don't believe that one's view of Hell (or limiting its duration) is a determining factor in salvation.

Although Universalists and those in Universal Reconciliation want to claim what they feel is the moral high ground on the topic of God's love (by saying "everyone will be saved"), they use the lightning rod of "rethinking Hell" like a flagpole on the hill where many of them choose to make their stand.

So . . . if Hell isn't the biggest issue, why am I writing a book that, in addition to other things, will devote so much text to the topic of punishment/Hell?

Because in order to *get* to their conclusions regarding Hell, Universalists present select words and verses from the Bible which can be read in such a way as to support their view. In doing so, they are (perhaps unintentionally) driving the topics of salvation, faith, our walk with God, and the ability to understand Scripture into a dead end. Although I don't do it with any sense of joy, I feel I *must* address their ideas on Hell (including the sheer weight of Scripture that contradicts their interpretations) in order to come to their conclusions. Much of what I will present to you is what they are NOT telling you, the things they are willing to set aside. When *anyone* (regarding *any* issue) uses a handful of Bible verses or a possible meaning of a single word in an attempt to overthrow a large amount of evidence stating the opposite . . . we should *all* take note.

What drives Universalist and Universal Reconciliation teaching?

1. I believe that part of what drove many Universalists in the past was their *reaction* to what they saw as the *unfairness* of a doctrine of "predestination" as it was defined in their denomination while they experienced, watched, or were asked to explain horrible situations in this world and had to say that God planned it that way. Many of them were ministers or strong teachers who spent a great deal of time working among people with tough questions about why people suffer and what happens to whole people groups who haven't ever seen a Bible or heard the Gospel. Since their denominational teachings on predestination offered little (if any) comfort, some eventually abandoned the effort of sharing the gospel and focused their ministry on love or service, saying this was all God requires.

2. In trying to explain how God can control *everything* in this world and still be defined as Love, some came to a crisis and eventually decided that He does control it all, but He will also save it all.

3. Others were in a denomination that said if you weren't a member of that denomination (and a partaker of specific rituals, rules, confessions, works, and structures—requiring much more than a simple belief in Christ) . . . well you just weren't *completely* saved. You could even be a devoted follower of the denomination every day of your life and *still* miss Heaven if you didn't get last rites or some other dispensation that would allow you into the Pearly Gates. I can see how that would get difficult to explain and practice after a while.

4. What seems to guide many of Universalism's *newer* teachers, however, is a focus on the icon of political correctness—thus the need to "include" everyone without requirements for personal faith in Jesus Christ or a need to follow Him in this life. According to them, salvation is an irresistible force that will prevail because, in essence, *no one is allowed to choose otherwise.* According to many teachers in Universalism, this eventual "reconciliation" includes all people, demons, and even Satan.

5. What drives a <u>small</u> number of them is the need for controversy. These are people who thrive on arguments. They relish (and *profit* from) the scandals they cause. Even if you could 100% prove them wrong, they would simply go out and find some other scandalous idea in order to put their faces in the public eye (and their books on your shelf).

But among who actually *believe* it, teachers of Universalism and UR <u>all</u> appear to be starting out with a <u>foundational assumption that salvation is *not* a matter of freewill, that it's all predetermined by God.</u> I don't wish to make predestination (a teaching that says mankind has no real choices, that God has "predestined" everything—Hyper-Calvinism) the main topic here—but it appears to be a fundamental *germinating* factor in Universal teaching, so I felt I had to acknowledge it here.

Since, in their view, there is no *question* of salvation, the focus of Universalists and those in UR shifts to limiting the terms of judgment or refuting the words about punishment and separation from God mentioned in the Bible. Their arguments are framed so as to question whether or not Christians today understand what God *intended* to say. As a support to their side of the debate, Universalists continually offer the idea that some Christians in the "first few Centuries" of the Church held Universalistic views, that these views were considered "important" and were accepted by "many."

Of note: Today's *followers* of Christian Universalism can be another group altogether. All of the ones I've known thus far seem to think they're the beta testers [v] for God's love:

Will you love me if I do THIS? How about if I do THAT? How about if I do it OVER HERE?

I have yet to meet a ("Christian") Universalist who has actually *studied* Universalism (or how it is derived). I have yet to meet one who wasn't truly tangled up with a need of a deep healing of some sort. (Confession: Unless I have time to back up and pray, I admit that their *spiritual tantrum* type of behavior and emotional decision making can vex the practical side of me pretty quickly. Hey—pray for me. I'm human, too!) HOWEVER, if you know/love one of these people, you would do well to follow Jesus' example in how He ministered to the woman at the well (John 4—I've written more about this in a few pages). Although Jesus was up front in saying He disagreed with her religious thoughts . . . He didn't take the bait of turning it into a debate. Instead, He chose to go for the deeper issue in her heart and minister to that.

There isn't a lot of value in arguing with the wounded about doctrines or folly. Be willing to speak about the Healer first, and know that if you can draw someone closer to Jesus, *He* is capable of leading them to eternal Truth (rather than slices of truths).

Develop a personal habit of sorting information

Before we allow alternate views (that some accept as Christian) open access to our lives, we need to start asking questions. Upon what do the appeals for redefining faith, salvation, and punishment rest? What has led people to the revelations they claim are found in Scripture? Is there evidence that the apostles and first century church embraced Universalism or Universal Reconciliation? *Are* the current translations of Scripture faulty? Is there a great storehouse of newly found writings of the apostles and first century Church leaders that could blow the lid off traditional thinking? Are there new archaeological discoveries that could clarify our vision of the past?

YOU are the one who must decide what or whom to believe, so I hope you will approach the subject of Universalism with a desire to know Jesus first and foremost, then weigh the claims against what Jesus Himself said, the record of what He did, what is found in the rest of Scripture, and what we can see in history.

Where Some Paths Diverged

Many of the darkest days of Christianity come when the Body (the Church) becomes separated from God's word. That separation can come—as it did in the dark ages—when poverty and ignorance create a vacuum and those who control the masses can remove the Bible from view. It can also come as those in the Body divorce themselves from the responsibility of knowing it for themselves and simply trust others to give them whatever today's lens lets those in power "see" there. Sadly, I think we may be on the verge of another of those dark times.

I have no doubt that people *can* get saved and seek to walk with God in the absence of Bibles . . . but the number of those who find Him and have abundant spiritual lives in Him is severely limited when God's word is hidden from view, or set aside.

---

[v] Beta testers are people who test software to see if it's functional under lots of different circumstances and try to find any flaws, points of failure, or bugs.

A foundation stone for many of the divergent theologies of today was brought forth in the thesis of one man, written in 1934. [vi] At the time it was written, the black curtain of Nazism held it away from the eyes of those outside Germany, the country where it was penned. After WWII, it remained, virtually forgotten, until a number of scholars and theologians were influenced by the work when it was translated into English in the 1970s. Inspired by the thesis, some of those scholars went on to claim that virtually nothing in Scripture can be proven or accepted as completely true, and that the history of traditional Christianity as we know it is wrong. This is despite the fact that the thesis was criticized by peers in 1930s within Germany, and again refuted by historians and Bible scholars when it was translated in the 1970s.

I don't know the political views of **Walter Bauer**, the man who wrote the original thesis but I do know that it was written during the darkest days of German history. At that time, in order to pull the German Church into his grasp, Hitler increasingly encouraged anything and everything that would cast doubt on the foundations of Christianity and the heredity of Jesus Christ—in order to sever or weaken the Church's dependence on the Bible. Those theologians and Christians who participated in (or at least didn't object to) the promotion of this thinking were not persecuted. (The eventual incarceration, torture, and murder of thousands who refused to bend to this view is well documented.) I won't attempt to demonize Mr. Bauer here. He may have just been a guy trying to get his degree by asking, a "What if?" kind of question.

The main thrust of Walter Bauer's paper, known as *the Bauer Thesis* was to say that there were *many* "forms of Christianity" in the beginning with widely divergent views and that the rising powerhouse of the Roman Church of the fourth century squelched everything that disagreed with them, then eliminated evidence of diverse and oppositional churches from the record and from Scriptures. His "proof" was that the record of many of these divergent communities *cannot* be found. Yes. You read that correctly. The proof he offered for his theory that there were widespread, wildly differing forms of Christianity in the early days of the church is: The fourth-century bullies of the church were so successful at destroying evidence . . . that little of it has been found.

Bauer himself *admitted* that his work was based upon speculation but decades later, those won over by the translation of Bauer's work during the freewheeling 1970s in Western culture took his ideas and ran with them. One of his staunchest followers, Bart Ehrman has written no less than four *New York Times* bestselling books that question the authenticity of the Bible and early Church history. This is no tiny tempest in a teapot! [vii] Clearly, in today's environment, controversy sells.

I want to be sure to note several things here. First of all, there are **many** highly educated historians and scholars who completely disagree with the Bauer thesis and the opinions of Bart Erhman. Secondly, while there IS historic evidence that points to a wide variety of "Christian"

---

vi Walter Bauer wrote *Rechtgläubigkeit und Ketzerei im ältesten Christentum* in 1934; Bauer developed his thesis that in earliest Christianity in many regions, (what we would now call) heresy was the original manifestation of Christianity. A second edition, edited by Georg Strecker, Tübingen was published in 1964, was translated in English as *Orthodoxy and Heresy in Earliest Christianity* in 1971,.

vii Although I didn't directly quote it here, many facts on this topic (as well as an overview of how the New Testament was compiled, and other data regarding early Church history) are available in the book, The Heresy of Orthodoxy, How Contemporary Culture's Fascination with Diversity Has Reshaped our Understanding of Early Christianity by Andreas J. Kostenberger and Michael J. Kruger published by Crossway Books in 2010. They decided to use "Heresy of Orthodoxy" reflecting that in today's atmosphere of political correctness, the only thing deemed heresy (unacceptable) is Orthodoxy. If you want to read up on the topics listed here and want a listing of many other resources, I recommend the book.

beliefs in the *third and fourth* centuries—this could hardly be referred to as diversity during the time of "the first Church." Next, consider that by the close of the first century, Christianity had been dispersed into the far corners of the known world. Selectively seeking and destroying apostolic writings and Church history from the first century wasn't as easy as pushing a *delete* button in some central computer server system. And finally, by the third century (where much of Universalism is rooted), a *lot* of things which the Bible forbids began to flourish in the church. To formulate any sort of template for Christianity and Christian life based on that era is, in my opinion, like trying to build something based upon a tenth generation photocopy of a photocopy that's been embellished by various people along the way.

But the growing glut of material questioning *everything* we've been taught from the Bible and Church history has led some to the conclusion that the entire New Testament (including what salvation really is, and how people come to salvation) is faulty.

The Responsibility of Christian Leadership, Now More than Ever:
Seeing the need of reasoning together

Something that has been lost in many denominations is the ability for the local Body to come together and actually *discuss* their faith, the Scriptures, and the issues—to *reason together* about these things. A "Bible Study" is often just more preaching—one person telling everyone what the selected verses mean and most of the gathered flock sitting in silence. How often I've heard pastors and teachers bemoan the fact that their people aren't "getting it" or living out the truths of the Bible. *Is it because the people sitting out there listening aren't involved in discovering and chewing these truths for themselves?* For the average believer, a Bible study is another opportunity to sit like a Christian couch potato. Occasionally, the people in the study are asked a question but most are afraid it's some sort of "trick question" and wouldn't dare respond. In some studies, people are given workbooks which list the scriptures to look up before penciling in a missing word or phrase in the slot provided. For the most part, nobody has asked the members of the church to actually *think* in years.

It's kind of like parents avoiding discussion of the topics of sex or drugs with their kids . . . with the mistaken idea that the lack of discussion will promote lack of dangerous behavior. Instead, their children hear it from some of the worst sources on the planet, and often let these bad sources determine what they do. The refusal of church leadership to have *meaningful dialog* with their congregations about critical issues surrounding faith has created a vacuum and left much of the flock open to false or misguided ideas.

The responsibility of ALL believers, now more than ever:
Each of us should know what (and Whom) we claim to believe.

Passivity and the need for popularity (fame) have done more to quench vitality in the Body of Christ than any totalitarian regime. We're used to just sitting and absorbing information. Taking in, taking in, taking in. We let polls validate what we think. We let Facebook "likes" determine who is the king of the moment. We sit listening to sermons and Bible Studies with our minds either distracted or entertained—but not engaged. We're not expected to respond with anything but an occasional "amen." All too often, there is no space, time, or *permission* given for honest give-and-take discussion.

There are LOTS of people in this world who know and can quote more Scripture than me, who can pray more, who can do more or do it better . . . but does that divorce me from my responsibility to love the Lord my God with all *my* heart, soul (mind) and strength? No it does not!

The only way the slide toward total numb relativism can stop is for ordinary people to take up "the good fight for the true faith." I'm not talking about each person deciding what they want the Bible to mean and planting a flag on that hill. I'm talking about praying together, about engaging our minds and *reasoning together* about what faith really is, what the Bible and the first Church can teach us about salvation and walking in faith.

The disciples whom Jesus first chose had little in the way of formal education. After Paul became a follower of Jesus Christ he was willing to set aside the studied hardness of his former life to teach the simplicity of the gospel to anyone who had an ear to hear. Over the centuries, scholars have labored (and many have given their very lives) to translate and deliver *to the ordinary men and women of the church* the message of the gospel of Jesus Christ. It was a message intended to be read and *grasped* by those who wouldn't let it be choked out by the cares, threats, or pleasures of this world. I pray this generation will take up that same cause.

> *Dear friends, although I was very eager to write to you about the salvation we share, I felt compelled to write and urge you to contend for the faith that was once for all entrusted to God's holy people.* [Jude 1: 3]

> *Pursue righteousness and a godly life, along with faith, love, perseverance, and gentleness. Fight the good fight for the true faith. Hold tightly to the eternal life to which God has called you, which you have confessed so well before many witnesses.* [1 Tim. 6:11b-12]

CHAPTER 2—The Call of Intergalactic Rabbit Trails
(The Questions that Keep People Up at Night)

Is God fair? How could a "loving" God let people in India starve? Do you expect us to believe God actually created the universe? What about the Crusades, the horrors of war, and the persecution of people groups?

I'm not a gospel tract kinda person. I'm not into doing the hard sell with the Roman Road or turning every conversation into a means of putting the gospel in someone's face. However, when the subject of faith *does* arrive in conversations, I often hear something about people in India who are starving, or the "inaccuracies" of the Bible, or about people who were killed in the Crusades . . . or how it's all just stories. But are these questions the actual issues? Or are they rabbit trails that keep people from thinking about what's *really* killing them? The rabbit trails are mental mazes which *rarely* end in rational solutions. **Often, what it's really about is where people feel God and/or the church has failed them personally.** It's about deep wounds . . . or loved ones lost in a tragedy . . . or an unwillingness to be surrounded by people with pointing fingers.

The Woman at the Well

In CHAPTER 4 of the Gospel of John we see a woman of Samaria. She is quite possibly the town's bad girl, and perhaps fearing the hard stares of other women in the village who went to get water in the cool of the day, she has gone alone to the well in the afternoon to draw water. She encounters a man (a Jew) who asks her to give him some water.

You have to understand, at this point in time, the Jews and Samaritans have been feuding for generations over *who* exactly is right with God. Samaritans, the ones who got stuck with the brand "unclean!" always seem to get the short end of the stick. Add to this the fact that no self-respecting Jewish man would remain in obvious proximity of a lone woman . . . especially not an unclean Samaritan woman. But here stands this guy in traditional Jewish garb, with no one else around, asking her to get him a drink.

If we were to put it in today's terms, in the mind of the Samaritan woman her status next to his would be seen like this:

If He ran a car dealership it would be Mercedes, and her old heap would be behind her shack with grass growing through it.

If he was like an Apple MacBook Pro, she would be seen as a wheezing old HP desktop with a pirated version of Microsoft Vista.

If he was a talent scout for the Miss Universe Pageant . . . she would be fat, dirty, and covered with scars.

You get the picture now?

So she immediately (verbally) sticks a sign in the ground with a big DETOUR arrow pointing in the direction of the first rabbit trail:

> 9 "You are a Jew and I am a Samaritan woman. How can *you* ask *me* for a drink?" (For Jews do not associate with Samaritans.)

Today's translation: *What's the likes of you doing in <u>this</u> neighborhood? What's the matter, your limo break down on the road outside of town? I may be an outcast of this village, but YOU are the bigger outcast here!*

He ignores the question.

> 10 Jesus answered her, "If you knew the gift of God and who it is that asks you for a drink, you would have asked him and he would have given you living water."

Real meaning: *You don't recognize me, but I'm not here to scorn you. I'm here to save you.*

A thought quickly comes to her. *Has anybody ever told this guy that he was born on the wrong side of the feud between Jews and Samaritans?* Another detour sign gets shoved into the ground:

> 11 "Sir," the woman said, "you have nothing to draw with and the well is deep. Where can you get this living water? 12 Are you greater than <u>our</u> father Jacob, who gave <u>us</u> the well and drank from it himself, as did also his sons and his livestock?"

Translation: *You Jews think that Jacob is your ancestor, but he's ours, too!*

Jesus doesn't go there.

> 13 Jesus answered, "Everyone who drinks this water will be thirsty again, 14 but whoever drinks the water I give them will never thirst. Indeed, the water I give them will become in them a spring of water welling up to eternal life."

Real meaning: *This isn't about history or genealogies, child; it's about <u>you</u>, this very moment.*

She's somewhat interested . . . but another thought pops into her brain. If an endless supply of this "water" would keep her from having to come to the well in the odd hours of the day, maybe she could stay isolated from the scorn of the village!

> 15 The woman said to him, "Sir, give me this water so that I won't get thirsty and have to keep coming here to draw water."

For Jesus, this isn't *really* about water. It's about life. And He wants to see if, despite her hurt and her outcast position (in the village and in the larger scheme of their world), is she willing to acknowledge some truth about herself?

> 16 He told her, "Go, call your husband and come back."

Ouch! . . . Now she can either lie to this stranger (who, for all she knows, will be gone soon and never know the difference) or she can just say it. Well, he hasn't seemed put off by the fact that she's a Samaritan or that she's a woman. Let's see what He does with *this* information! If nothing else, they can fight over whether or not she's living in sin!

> 17 "I have no husband," she replied.
>
> Jesus said to her, "You are right when you say you have no husband. 18 The fact is, you have had five husbands, and the man you now have is not your husband. What you have just said is quite true."

Jesus affirms her truthful response . . . and reveals that he knows things he couldn't know unless he was a deeply spiritual man. Intriguing! But, if he's a godly man, he might touch on the things that are *really* killing her. Time for the next detour sign!

> 19 "Sir," the woman said, "I can see that you are a prophet. 20 Our ancestors worshiped on this mountain, but you Jews claim that the place where we must worship is in Jerusalem."

Real meaning: *Let's get into a religious debate! We could go 'round and 'round for hours about the spot that God really chose for worship. In the process we could offend one another and then avoid each other (and the more important question) permanently!*

But Jesus separates what's important (life giving) from what is a distraction.

> 21 "Woman," Jesus replied, "believe me, a time is coming when you will worship the Father neither on this mountain nor in Jerusalem. 22 You Samaritans worship what you do not know; we worship what we do know, for salvation is from the Jews. 23 Yet a time is coming and has now come when the true worshipers will worship the Father in the Spirit and in truth, for they are the kind of worshipers the Father seeks. 24 God is spirit, and his worshipers must worship in the Spirit and in truth."

He's making a radical statement about worship (it will be done everywhere!) but He's also testing her openness. He's telling her the truth about her religious beliefs. Is she interested in *truly* entering into worship? Does she *want* to know God? Is eternal life (what she cannot fully see or grasp) more important than the worldly issues that seem to dog her every step?

> 25 The woman said, "I know that Messiah" (called Christ) "is coming. When he comes, he will explain everything to us."

She has just made a small statement of faith ("I know the Messiah is coming") that reflects what she believes. Jesus sees that her heart is open, so He tells her the Truth.

> 26 Then Jesus declared, "I, the one speaking to you—I am he."

We don't know how long they talked, but one verse later in the story we see the beginning of her choice for *eternal* water, and a new life for her.

28 Then, <u>leaving her water jar</u>, the woman went back to the town and said to the people, 29 "Come, see a man who told me everything I ever did. Could this be the Messiah?" 30 They came out of the town and made their way toward him.

A few verses later:

39 Many of the Samaritans from that town <u>believed in him because of the woman's testimony</u>, "He told me everything I ever did." 40 So when the Samaritans came to him, they urged him to stay with them, and he stayed two days. 41 And because of his words many more became believers.

42 They said to the woman, "<u>We no longer believe just because of what you said; now we have heard for ourselves, and we know that this man really is the Savior of the world.</u>"

There it is in a nutshell. This woman experienced something and her testimony of it brought others into the presence of Jesus, but once there, they came to believe for themselves.

Issues to chew on:

1) Her little evangelistic crusade wasn't the result of training or following a prescribed formula, it was a joyous outflow of something that had taken place within her.
2) Something *discernible* had happened to the woman, something compelling enough to bring people out to see Jesus, where they could get to know Him for themselves.
3) Does God force people to believe who He is? Should <u>we</u> attempt to force them?
4) What does it mean to be "the Savior of the <u>world</u>"?

CHAPTER 3—Why *did* Jesus come to Earth?

Beginning at the Beginning

The following is NOT a debate as to whether or not Adam and Eve actually existed. I happen to believe they did, but regardless of my (or your) opinion in the matter, IF you believe that God gave us the Scriptures—then you believe that He gave us this story in order that we might LEARN something about who He is and how He accomplishes what He does. So indulge me a moment and think about a few things.

Once upon a time a man and woman were in a garden of perfection. There was beauty, innocence, satisfying work, and an open relationship with God. There was only *one* thing God asked them NOT to do. . . . Eat from the tree of the knowledge of good and evil.

In Genesis, we see the encounter between the woman and the serpent in the garden:

> **Genesis 3:1-3** Now the serpent was more crafty than any of the wild animals the LORD God had made. He said to the woman, "Did God <u>really</u> say, 'You must not eat from any tree in the garden'?"
>
> The woman said to the serpent, "We may eat fruit from the trees in the garden, but God did say, 'You must not eat fruit from the tree that is in the middle of the garden, and you must not touch it, or you will die.' "

Stop! Let's back up the truck here! *Did* God say they couldn't <u>touch</u> the tree? . . . If we turn back one page to Genesis 2:15-17, God simply says that they weren't to <u>eat</u> from the tree, and we see no commands about not touching it. So . . . why did the woman say that? Whether this was something Adam told her or it was something she thought of herself, one or both of them thought it necessary to *add* to God's commands—and as soon as the woman said this, the serpent knew he had an advantage. If God's command was in need of a fence, if God couldn't be simply taken at His word, why not cast further doubt on what God said? *Was* God telling the truth or was He just trying to keep them from something wonderful?

> **Genesis 3:4-5** "You will not surely die," the serpent said to the woman. "For God knows that when you eat of it your eyes will be opened, and you will be like God, knowing good and evil."

Since the beginning, Satan has been helping people to question the Lord's character, His love, and the meaning of His words. Since the beginning, Satan has taken on the task of disputing God's warnings.

Satan wanted to plant several false assumptions in Eve's mind. Via half-truths, he hoped to appeal to her emotions and desires. Here are his implications:

1) God's words aren't to be taken literally. You won't <u>die</u> (today, physically. Satan was playing a game with a possible meaning of the word "die" for his own purposes.)
2) Denying you the fruit of that tree is so unfair. How could a *loving* God keep you in the dark like this?
3) God wants to withhold something good from you.
4) Godhood is attainable (and then, what would you need <u>Him</u> for?)

Waiter! She wants the whole enchilada, with an order of godhood on the side, please!— Make that To Go!

The woman chose to ignore God's warning based on the serpent's word games, her false assumptions, emotions, and desires. It was very costly. When she ate the fruit she _didn't_ immediately (physically) die . . . but something _did_ happen. She became aware of . . . shame—the ultimate intimacy stealer when it comes to relating to God. The sheer joy of innocence and beauty she found in Father God's presence was suddenly and permanently snapped; making the first death she experienced her spiritual death. She might have been "like God" in the way of knowing something was wrong, but I'm sure that this wasn't what she had in mind.

And, we've all heard it, misery loves company . . . so she gave some of the fruit to Adam and he ate it.

God soon confronted them with their sin, made them exit the garden, and blocked mankind's reentry. Why? Because Adam, Eve, and the seed within them—all the generations to come—were now unable to stand with God in innocence. Their open connection with God was lost, and this loss would be passed on from generation to generation. Rather than have them eat of the tree of Life and live perpetually in their shame, unable to communicate with Him face to face—God banned them from Eden. They moved into the world, now under the dominion of Satan (to whom they had yielded authority over humankind when they ate) and eventually they both died physically.

FROM THE BEGINNING, people were given a choice involving taking God at His word or choosing their own path (which they were told would lead to death). This choice is offered repeatedly throughout Scripture and is still being offered today.

What did _we_ lose in the Garden? And what does it mean to say that Jesus is the Savior of the World?

The day that Adam and Eve chose the knowledge of good and evil over their relationship with God, _all of humanity_ lost connectivity with God (the spirit of man died, closing down open communion with the Spirit of God). We also forfeited our place of governance in the world. In the Gospel of John, the Greek word _kosmos_ is found seventy-five times. Although the word is translated "world" it mostly refers to the governance of things, the spiritual, social, and political structures of life here. When Adam and Eve fell, they handed over the structure that governs life on earth.[viii]

After the fall, humanity was disconnected, physically mortal, spiritually dead, and under the influence of Satan. But even in the midst of pronouncing punishment for their disobedience in the garden, God gave a promise: That the "seed" of the woman (Jesus) would eventually crush the head of the serpent (Genesis 3:15) who is Satan (Revelation 12:9)

God's promise was that someone would come and reopen the access between God and humans. A man, born of a woman would come to make a way of escape from under Satan's dominion.

Did Jesus come here merely to take a punishment or to pay a ransom?

If you're interested, take some time one day and just look at the accounting terms used in scripture: Ransom, Reconcile, Reckon, Count, Redeem, Paid.

---

viii Jack W. Hayford, General Editor, Hayford's Bible Handbook, ©1995 Thomas Nelson Inc., Nashville, Tennessee, see pp. 314 and 316

Jesus paid a price for us which we couldn't pay for ourselves. It isn't about just taking a terrible beating and then dying, it's about leaving His throne—all the glories of Heaven that were *already* His—and divesting Himself of EVERYTHING to come in the flesh, *in person*, and settle OUR account. Jesus paid the cost of our ransom. There is no other payment you can make *instead* of the ransom that He paid. It was paid on behalf of ALL humanity, it is *offered* to all, and God accepts no other payment from you.

(I'm one of those people who scribbles notes and uses highlighters all over books, so I tried to provide some blank spaces here and there within the book and **I hope you will highlight / write your own notes** all over the place as you read.)

CHAPTER 4—Introduction to a Mystery! The debate over meaning

Picture it: One hundred years from now, a man is restoring an old house that was built centuries ago. Under a layer of flooring, he finds a scrap of paper. The fragment is brown and it nearly crumbles in his hand. He carefully carries it into the light and gently sets it on a table where he can just make out the following words:

> *they make Constance fast,*
>
> *girding her about*
>
> *against angry tides and stout men.*

So who is Constance? What is this all about? He begins to ponder it . . .

Because he loves horses, the man's first thought is that Constance could be a horse—a swift runner. The "they" could apply to the special diet and training her handlers gave her. But the scrap of paper holding these words looks old, and in ye olde English, the term "make fast" could mean to tie something (as with a rope). The word "girding" might imply a saddle of some sort that helped her to carry a "stout" (stalwart) rider into the fierce tides of battle.

But, given the word "tides" in the sentence, Constance could have been a ship—and "fast" might refer to her speed at sea (in the "angry tides"). Or she might have been "tied" to a dock or buoy so she wouldn't drift away in the tides. To further the idea that Constance might be a ship, there were times when ancient mariners would "gird" their ships to help hold them together or to help keep a large patch on a leak. "Stout men" might be a reference to pirates or strong men . . . or sailors who were full of "stout" (beer). *Arrg!*

But Constance *could* be a woman. And the name Constance means "steadfast"—so the word "fast" here might be some sort of play on words regarding her name. Constance was the name of a daughter of the Emperor Constantine, as well as a daughter of William the Conqueror, and a wife of Henry VI, so maybe this is about someone of royal lineage standing firm during an uprising!

Another idea: In the early to mid-1900s, a "fast" woman was a woman of ill repute. Perhaps, having been so worldly, Constance learned to emotionally shut down and guard herself against the hard realities of this world, thus "girding" herself against the ebb and flow of angry drunks in her life.

OR, maybe Constance was a fashion model in the 1980s who was forced to "fast" (not eat) and she tightened her belt to keep her from succumbing to hunger in the mall where fat people moved about like an angry sea of humanity.

Then again . . .

All this is plenty to consider. But add to the mix the complication of *where* this fragment comes from. Is this a line from a poem? Is it an eye-witness account? A part of a novel? A letter from a king? When was it written? To whom was it written?

If all I have is this one fragment floating alone on a tabletop . . . I can make it mean nearly anything I want it to mean. Just think what a lawyer, or a salesman, or a politician could do with it! Whole books could be written about Constance the horse, or Constance the ship, or Constance the naughty woman, or Constance the starving model, or how we must treat all women with the name Constance.

This is but a small example of the need for context when we want to discover true meaning. IT'S THE SAME PROBLEM we encounter when we only read/study select verses of the Bible that have been plucked from their context and set on a table like the fragment of paper in the illustration above. When we allow people to "prove" their point with a verse of scripture or the possible definition of a single word, each removed from the framework in which they were placed, we can find ourselves "believing" something that may have been stripped of its true meaning. Are you willing to hang the entire weight of your life upon someone's speculation? I'm not.

So let us look together at some of Universalism's current teachings about death and the afterlife. Let's see where or if their ideas are found within the context of the whole Bible, the words of Jesus, and the actions of God.

I'll warn you that being willing to look at what actually is or isn't in the Bible regarding any given topic involves risk on your part because there will be times when the whole council of God's word doesn't gibe with something you've been taught your whole life, or it will contradict something you want to see . . . and then you must decide what to believe.

CHAPTER 5—Death, Heaven, Hell, and the Resurrection

What does it mean when we say someone has "Passed away," entered "the big sleep," is "no longer with us" . . . a.k.a. DEAD?

Wow. Talk about a happy topic, eh? :-) But it's probably why you're reading this book, so let's get to it.

What does it mean when we say a person has died? Are they just . . . gone? Passed into non-existence? According to an international poll conducted by *Ipsos/Reuters* in 2011,[ix] less than a quarter of people in the world believe that death is final—that when you die, you simply cease to exist. More than half of the people (of all types of faiths, cultures, and nationalities polled) however, thought that the soul of a person would go on after death. A simple way most *Christians* would describe it would be to say that the soul of the person has ceased to inhabit a physical body. (According to a 2011 *Gallup* poll, more than nine out of ten Americans still believe there is a God[x] who presumably watches over us, even in death).

The debate comes when we speak of *where* the *soul*[xi] of each person will end up, *how* they will get there, and how long they'll stay in that place.

What does the Bible say happens when people die? Where do they go? From the perspective of the *Old Testament*, even righteous people who died *didn't* go to "Heaven." Really.

According to the Bible (until the resurrection[xii] of Jesus) the souls of everyone who died went to what the Jews referred to (in general) as Sheol, the grave, the place of the dead—but even before the time of Jesus, many Jews believed there was a division between those who were right with God, and those who were not. The "righteous" dead were said to be in "Paradise" which was also called "Abraham's Bosom." The unrighteous dead were said to be in "Hades" (also called "Gehenna.") Both the place for the righteous (Abraham's Bosom/Paradise) and the unrighteous (Hades/Gehenna) were considered "down" (below the ground). This concept is supported in Deuteronomy 32:22; Amos 9:2; Psalm 9:17; Psalm 49:14; Isaiah 14 and Proverbs 14:32. [xiii]

---

ix The Ipsos/Reuters poll posted in the *Christian Post*, read more at http://www.christianpost.com/news/global-poll-most-believe-in-god-afterlife-49994/#MIxDTSxpyCz8Y5lO.99

x 2011 Gallup Poll on belief in God, http://www.gallup.com/poll/147887/americans-continue-believe-god.aspx

[xi] **The term "soul"** used here is a reference to the personality, will, mind desire, and awareness of a person (what makes you *you*) that exists beyond the death of the body. See Matt. 10: 28, Matt. 22:37, 2 Cor. 5:8, Rev. 6:9, Rev. 20:4

[xii] **The term "resurrection"** although it can apply to someone being resuscitated (in a body that will still age and perish, such as Lazarus in John 11), when it is applied to the future of *humanity* refers to the event when each soul will a) receive a new, imperishable body like Jesus already has [eternal life] OR, b) when the soul will be brought to stand before the Lord for judgment [condemnation]. Jesus was the *first* resurrected being and He is the only one with an immortal, resurrected body right now.

xiii Fausset, Andrew R. *Faussett's Bible Dictionary*, Public Domain

In Luke 16, Jesus tells the story of a poor beggar by the name of Lazarus who died and went "to Abraham's Bosom" and of a rich man who ignored Lazarus in life, then died and went to "Hades." Jesus says that Lazarus was comforted for all the sorrows he knew on earth but the other man was in torment. The (formerly) rich man begged Abraham to let Lazarus give him something to drink but Abraham told him that there was a fixed chasm between the two places (dividing righteous and unrighteous) that *no one* could cross it.

Who is in Heaven now?

When Jesus was on the cross, he told one of the thieves being crucified next to Him, "Today, you will be with me in Paradise." (Luke 23:43) Since Jesus wouldn't be resurrected and ascend to Heaven for three more days, this was not a reference to Heaven, but to Abraham's Bosom (in the earth).

In the book of Ephesians, Paul refers to Jesus "descending" (into the earth) and "ascending" (into Heaven).

> **Ephesians 4:7-10** "But to each one of us grace was given according to the measure of Christ's gift. Therefore it says,
> "When He ascended on high,
> He led captive a host of captives,
> And He gave gifts to men."
> (Now this expression, "He ascended," what does it mean except that He also had descended into the lower parts of the earth? He who descended is Himself also He who ascended far above all the heavens, so that He might fill all things.)"*—end quote. *Note: all of this, including the question in parenthesis is in the NASB Bible.*

> In the indented text, Paul is quoting Psalm 68:18

> * Some Christians read these verses in Ephesians as merely stating that Jesus descended to earth, paid the ransom to set captives (us) free, then went to Heaven, mission accomplished. Either way, after Jesus ascended to Heaven, the word Paradise became another word used in Scripture for Heaven *above* us (2 Cor. 12:2-4, Rev. 2:7).

Jesus Christ rose from the grave in a resurrected (immortal, glorified) body and ascended into Heaven. Many Christians believe the above verse in Ephesians is saying that Jesus descended INTO the earth, then took with Him all the souls of those who were in Paradise/Abraham's Bosom—He emptied Abraham's Bosom when He ascended into Heaven.

What other clue is there that might point to this idea? The writer of Hebrews names saints (even some of those from the Old Testament), and describes them as, now being in a great "cloud" of witnesses (above):

> **Hebrews 12:1-2** Therefore, since we are surrounded by such a great cloud of witnesses, let us throw off everything that hinders and the sin that so easily entangles. And let us run with perseverance the race marked out for us, 2 fixing our eyes on Jesus, the pioneer and perfecter of faith. For the joy set before him he endured the cross, scorning its shame, and sat down at the right hand of the throne of God.

After Jesus ascended to Heaven, the Way to the Father was open. When a righteous person dies, their soul is with the Lord, awaiting the resurrection, when they will be given immortal bodies. Paul

---

<http://www.studylight.org/dic/fbd/view.cgi?number=T1605>

the apostle compared the *earthly* (perishable) bodies of the righteous to houses or tents where our souls temporarily abide until they go home to be "with the Lord."

> **2 Corinthians 5:4-8** For indeed while we are in this tent, we groan, being burdened, because we do not want to be unclothed but to be clothed, so that what is mortal will be swallowed up by life. 5 Now He who prepared us for this very purpose is God, who gave to us the Spirit as a pledge.
>
> 6 Therefore, being always of good courage, and knowing that while we are at home in the body we are absent from the Lord—7 for we walk by faith, not by sight—8 we are of good courage, I say, and prefer rather to be absent from the body and to be at home with the Lord.

In addition, if we look in the book of Revelation 6:9, we see "the souls" of those who have been martyred crying out from beneath the altar of God (in Heaven), and in Revelation 7:9 we see a number of people which no man can number before the throne of God, and descriptions of "saints" in Heaven. So, according to the Bible, there are people in Heaven right now. Is *everyone* who has died in Heaven? Will everyone eventually get there? Let's give that some thought and study.

Rethinking the Traditional Concepts of Heaven and Hell

Quite a few people (even those who aren't Christians) have thoughts about Heaven and Hell— where these places are, what they are, what they might look like, and who goes where. But even if we just stick with what is voiced among Christians, let's just say the opinions still cover a wide spectrum.

Picturing HEAVEN—According to the World

If you were raised in Western culture, you've already been imprinted with our general ideas of Heaven and Hell. Many of us were given the idea that if we were "good" (our good deeds outweighing our misdeeds) then we would go to Heaven. We were told that "bad" people went to Hell. I wasn't raised in a Christian home and yet even *I* was exposed to these concepts as a child. The viewpoint is, indeed, found in a couple of small passages from the Bible:

> **John 5:28-29** "Do not be amazed at this, for a time is coming when all who are in their graves will hear his voice 29 and come out—<u>those who have done what is good will rise to live, and those who have done what is evil will rise to be condemned.</u>"

> **2 Corinthians 5:10** For we must all appear before the judgment seat of Christ, so that each one may be recompensed for his deeds in the body, according to what he has done, whether good or bad.

Even though the words of Jesus are in the first quote and Paul the apostle is speaking in the second . . . to lift them out of context is to let the world say "good works" will get you to Heaven— but this idea isn't in harmony with the message of the Gospel.

A slightly more *Christian-esque* picture of Heaven is to say that it's a place where people (who were "good"—went to church, read their Bibles, etc. in their earthly lives) will eternally float on clouds wearing white robes, playing harps. (And, often, this totally vanilla view is scoffed at by people who want to think of Heaven as a "boring" place.) Again, going to church, reading your Bible, etc. may be good things, but they won't *earn* you entrance to Heaven.

And if you ask people today, many will say they believe in "heaven" but then go on to say that it can be whatever a person wants it to be—like if you love art, Heaven would be a light-filled studio where you could endlessly splash whole new spectrums of color on canvas. No Scripture I know of says that we are the ones who determines what Heaven will look like or be like.

In Hollywood's versions of the afterlife, people work their way into angel-hood, trying to "earn their wings" by proving themselves worthy in some manner. This is not a scriptural concept at all since angels were created to be angels, people were created to be people . . . and there is no evidence that one can *work* one's way up through society in Heaven, or that you can "earn" <u>anything</u> once you've entered the afterlife.

So, what does Heaven look like in the Bible?

The truth is, **very little (that can be plainly understood) is said in the Bible about what Heaven will look or be like.** Before that casts a shadow of doubt in your heart as to the existence of Heaven, let me add an important point to note: One of the starkest differences between the faith depicted in the Bible and other beliefs was that God provided no images for people to worship / adore / focus on. God never wanted us to equate limited images to Him or to think we could somehow "contain" Him in a locale. Among tribal nations, the God of the Jews wasn't an object they could point to and say, "This is our God." Whenever the Jews *thought* they had God in a box (in the Ark of the Covenant, the temple, or even the city of Jerusalem) and they began to figure that this would ensure their prosperity regardless of what they did . . . they were brought to disaster. Jehovah was and IS the Living God—and He is *everywhere*.

Consistent with these facts we see that there are *no* detailed descriptions of what Jesus looked like in the New Testament. There wasn't even a cross or a crucifix on the wall where people first assembled to worship Him. The great I AM isn't contained in an object.

The few descriptions of Heaven in the Bible (whether they are symbolic or actual) tell us that it will be far grander than anything man has ever built—and completely illuminated with His glory. Whether or not the streets are actually paved with gold, or the sea is made of crystal, or its gates and walls are made of pearls and gems . . . I think God was trying to convey to us that Heaven is much MORE than we can imagine. Think of it—what people would kill for *here* is described as mere pavement there. And, even better than being in this beautiful place, WE will be completely whole, without spot or blemish, and able to see Jesus face to face. Scripture promises we will in some way be "like Him" but doesn't elaborate on what that entails.

So, it is consistent with the Lord's nature to NOT provide us with volumes of pictures of what Heaven (or even we) will look like—because Heaven is beyond description. And far outstripping anything we can *see* there, the essence, the sheer joy of Heaven will be in *standing* in the unveiled presence of God. Here is what Fausset's Bible Dictionary has to say about Heaven:

> The Bible is distinguished from the sacred books of false religions in not having minute details of heavenly bliss such as men's curiosity would crave. The grand feature of its blessedness is represented as consisting in holy personal union and immediate face to face communion with God and the Lamb; secondarily, that the saints are led by the Lamb to living fountains of water, and fed with the fruit of the tree of life in the midst of the paradise of God, the antitype of the former Adamic paradise.

> It is no longer merely a garden as Eden, but a heavenly "city" and garden combined, nature and art no longer mutually destructive, but enhancing each the charm of the other, individuality and society realized perfectly (Revelation 2-3, 7, 21-22). No separate temple, but

the whole forming one vast "temple," finding its center in the Lord God Almighty and the Lamb, who are the temple to each and all the king-priests reigning and serving there. [xiv]

For someone to try to "win" people to the Lord through descriptions of the glories of Heaven is probably no better than trying to scare people into the Kingdom by describing Hell (as the place they want to avoid)—for we must love God for who HE is, not merely for what we can get (or escape from). HE is *worthy* of our love, attention, adoration.

Yes, Jesus spoke often of the Kingdom of God and the Kingdom of Heaven—and His words reflected the fact that our hearts and minds can abide in its peace right *now*. In Heaven may be the full revelation of God and His kingdom, but when we decide to follow Jesus, our spirits are made alive and our souls have *already* become citizens of the Kingdom of Heaven, and we are to walk this earth *with Him* until He calls us Home. The pie-in-the-sky teaching that places Heaven at the center of focus has led some people to live empty lives that are of no earthly good. Jesus spoke with immediacy, about "today" and "now." He asks us to have faith now, hear His voice now, put His words into practice today (while you're here on this earth), help your neighbor now, work while it is yet day (today), forgive today, pray right now . . . and trust Him for tomorrow. THIS is consistent with God's words and His ways.

Picturing HELL—From a Traditional Standpoint

As their ideas take clearer shape, many within the Universal / UR movement say they want all Christians to rethink the idea of Hell. Well . . . okay. But before we can RE-think something we have to give it some actual thought in the first place, right?

The "common man's" view of Hell often consists of fire and devils in red costumes with horns and pitchforks. There are volumes of stories and jokes about Hell that, while they depict something terrible, also make it out as not such a bad place because it won't be boring (compared to their view of Heaven, where people just stand on clouds and play harps).

The "traditional" Protestant view of Hell pretty much says that if you haven't received Jesus as your savior, you are going to a place of eternal torment called Hell. In it are found fire and brimstone and misery. There will be no rest or comfort in Hell, nor will there be any escape from it. The Roman Catholic Church also teaches that there is an eternal Hell and that those who die *outside* God's grace and friendship are "condemned" and go there forever.

Actually, the Bible says more about Hell and judgment than about Heaven (and, to me, this is a clue that Hell is real . . . and that God *doesn't* want you to go there). I will quote a number of Scriptures on Hell, death and the lake of fire later in this chapter, but I first want to address an idea that I believe has played a foundational role in the *Universalist's* view of Hell: Within Roman Catholicism, they believe not only in Heaven and Hell, but *another* place called "purgatory." Here is the definition of purgatory from the website *Catholic Answers:*

> The Catechism of the Catholic Church defines purgatory as a "purification, so as to achieve the holiness necessary to enter the joy of heaven," which is experienced by those "who die in God's grace and friendship, but still imperfectly purified" (CCC 1030). It notes that "this final purification of the elect . . . is entirely different from the punishment of the damned." [xv]

---

xiv Fausset, Andrew R. Entry for "Heaven," *Fausset's Bible Dictionary*. Public Domain <http://www.studylight.org/dic/fbd/view.cgi?number=T1605>.

So, as I understand it, Roman Catholics believe there is a place called *purgatory*, and that it is a place of temporary but final purification for those who die "in God's grace and friendship" but are in need of further purification.

In Universalism, Hell is less like "traditional" Hell, More like Purgatory

"Christian Universalism," Universal Reconciliation and Universal Restoration, as I understand them, seem to have *replaced* the concept of Hell with purgatory—a place of temporary refining or purification. But Universalists and those in UR have *further* modified the idea of this purgatory-like Hell to include *anyone* who *at any time* may have fallen short of (Universalism's vague requirements for) Heaven. Most Universalists even include Satan and demons in the list of those who will undergo this refining process. They speak of this version of Hell as a time of "divine chastisement" that has no time limit (even though they say it's not eternal), and it will result in *everyone* eventually being welcomed into Heaven. I can see how Universalists find support from selected traditions of Roman Catholicism (and from some Catholics themselves). Both Christian Universalists and Roman Catholics emphasize tradition (such as the teachings of Origen) in their teachings on the afterlife—with many of them holding *tradition* as equal to or *above* Scripture. I find this a wee bit of an irony since so many Universalists are trying to shake off what they see as the stogy "traditional" ideas of Protestants.

As we consider this concept of a purgatory-*ish* Hell where everyone will eventually make bail, let's first think about whether or not the Bible tells us if someone can die in their sin (as Jesus said some Pharisees would) and merely undergo some method of "purification" after death that would cleanse them. What determines "saved"? Can people who totally reject God in this life still receive a cleansing after death which will save them? Do they get this purification/cleansing in *another* existence or as disembodied souls? Universal Reconciliation brings all these questions into the mix.

I'm willing to hear other viewpoints of Scripture, but so far as I know, you are either saved or you're not. The Bible says that when one who knows (has intimate fellowship with) Jesus Christ dies, they are present with Him—and Jesus is in Heaven.

Hell is "not eternal"? . . . And it's a "temporary place of *Divine reform*"?

That's what Universalists are saying. Could it be true? Could most Christians have just misunderstood the Bible all this time? Let's look at some examples where Universalists see this concept of Divine reform.

> **Matthew 25:46** [Jesus speaking] "Then they will go away to eternal punishment, but the righteous to eternal life."

In context, Jesus started this segment by talking about the judgment/separation of the "*sheep*" (whom He then says are His people) from the "*goats*" (those who are "cursed" and will be sent away). The verse above is the last sentence in the parable.

Referencing what Jesus said here about the goats, Rob Bell, in his book *Love Wins*, says that in the Greek language, the goats are being sent to an "*aion* of *kolazo*."[xvi] (Which as far as I know, is not completely accurate, but we'll get to that in a moment.)

---

xv "Purgatory" (CCC 1031), *Catholic Answers*, http://www.catholic.com/tracts/purgatory, (July12, 2012)

xvi Rob Bell, *Love Wins, A Book About Heaven, Hell, and the Fate of Every Person Who Ever Lived*, (New York

He goes on to say that one of the meanings of the Greek word "aion" is "age" or "period of time" and that the word "*kolazo*" can refer to "intensity of experience." He then extrapolates this to say that an *aion* of *kolazo*—instead of "eternal punishment" as it is translated in most English versions of the Bible, might really only be a "period of pruning" (thus introducing the idea that Hell is temporary and redemptive). He then declares that "'forever' is not really a category the biblical writers used."[xvii]

If you don't know who Rob Bell is, until 2011 he was a *very* popular pastor/teacher among young adults, made many DVD's and wrote a number of books on a variety of topics, coming from a sort of cool-post-modern-Christian-with-a-taste-for-controversy perspective.

Although we will talk about the word "aion" in Chapter Seven, the Greek word in this passage is not "aion" as Mr. Bell says, but "aionios." The word we *will* address right now is "*kolazo*" (which he says could mean "pruning") but it is *also not* in this passage of the Bible. The word in this passage is related to *kolazo*, it's "*kolasis*."

Referencing this same verse, the Christian Universalist Association (CUA) does correctly note the Greek word "*kolasis*," but they come to pretty much the same conclusion as Rob Bell. On the CUA page entitled *Divine Justice and Life After Death* [xviii] the claim is made that the "Bible makes clear that the purpose of 'hell' or suffering is not to torture people, but to cause them to learn from their mistakes and grow closer to perfection." They say that God's judgment is "reformative, not vindictive," and that the Greek word *kolasis*, used in Matthew 25:46 indicates "a beneficial chastening such as a gardener prunes a vine to remove dead vegetation and make it grow more."

Points to ponder:

First of all, we encounter the problem with the context. This is about goats, and we don't "prune" goats—we prune plants. Even if we set that aside, Universalists want you to believe that the intense "cutting back" of people *after death* will save them or help them *realize* they are saved and bear good fruit. But *where* would they produce this fruit? *What kind of fruit?* Are we to simply take the word of those in the Universal Reconciliation movement that people who hated God in this life, after being severely chastened for a "period of time" in Hell will somehow, eventually, learn to love Him, and "bear good fruit"?

There *are* things the Bible makes "clear" but using the Greek word *kolasis* to prove that the purpose of Hell is mere "chastening" or "pruning" is mistaken at best. The impression you might get from the statements made by Rob Bell and the CUA (and others in the UR movement) is that the New Testament is filled with uses of this word *kolasis* which demonstrate the concept of "beneficial chastening." But the Greek word *kolasis* is only used TWICE in the New Testament. Here are the two verses in which it appears:

> **Matt. 25:46** [Jesus speaking] "Then they will go away to eternal punishment (*kolasis*), but the righteous to eternal life." [NIV—Greek word placed in parenthesis by me]

HarperCollins Publishers 2011) 91-92.

xvii Rob Bell, Love Wins, A Book About Heaven, Hell, and the Fate of Every Person Who Ever Lived, (New York HarperCollins Publishers 2011) 91-92.

xviii On the page entitled "Divine Justice and Life After Death" linked from the "Statement of Faith" page on the website for The Christian Universalist Assoc. http://www.christianuniversalist.org/articles/justice-afterlife.html (13 October 2011)

> **1 John 4:18** There is no fear in love. But perfect love drives out fear, because fear has to do with punishment (*kolasis*). The one who fears is not made perfect in love. [NIV—*Greek word placed in parenthesis by me—and by the way, it seems to contradict the idea that punishment would make one perfect.*]

Now let's consider the Greek word, *kolasis*, translated "punishment" in the New International Version. In *context*, I don't believe "beneficial chastening" or "pruning" is even *implied* here—especially not in the context of the whole chapter of Matthew 25. (And I invite readers to read the entire chapter of Matthew 25 where Jesus discusses His return, describing it in three parables, and see if you think He was even *hinting* that the punishment of the wicked would be "restorative".)

If you look *kolasis* up Strong's Exhaustive Concordance of the Bible, you'll see it is, in fact, a derivative of the word *kolazo* which does mean "to lop or prune, as trees and wings, to curb, check, restrain, to chastise, correct, punishment, to cause to be punished."[xix] Bell and others are using the definition of *kolazo* to prove their point, but that isn't the word in the passage—the word used in both Matthew and 1 John is *kolasis,* and it means "penal infliction:—punishment, torment."[xx]

But let's look at a place in the Gospels where Jesus speaks metaphorically of plants. He compares Himself to the vine, and says people are the branches.

> **John 15:4-7** "Abide in Me, and I in you. As the branch cannot bear fruit of itself unless it abides in the vine, so neither can you unless you abide in Me. 5 I am the vine, you are the branches; he who abides in Me and I in him, he bears much fruit, for apart from Me you can do nothing. 6 <u>If anyone does not *abide* in Me, he is thrown away as a branch and dries up; and they gather them, and cast them into the fire and they are burned</u>. 7 If you abide in Me, and My words abide in you, ask whatever you wish, and it will be done for you."—NASB

The word translated "abide" here is the Greek word *meno* which means "to remain, not depart, to tarry, to continue to be present, to endure."[xxi] This word appears thirty-three times in the gospel of John alone (one hundred eighteen times in the whole New Testament)—*and where it is applied to our faith or our walk with God, it is always connected to a physical presence here on earth.*

In an attempt at making a metaphor that supports "divine chastening," Bell has totally missed the words of Jesus, who compares those who "abide" (follow, remain, continue) in Him in this life to the branches that remain attached to a plant and bear fruit—then compares the people *who don't abide in Him to branches that are thrown away, gathered up, and cast into the fire*.

Lastly, I want to show you a word that *is* translated both "chastening" and discipling in the New Testament—*paideuo* [Strong's #3811].[xxii] This word is used thirteen times and *none* of the uses of the word place God's "chastening" in the realm of the afterlife. The following passage serves as an excellent example of the difference between the "chastening" of the Lord in the life of a believer as opposed to the punishment awaiting those who are of this world:

[xix] "*kolazo*" Strong's #2949, James Strong, Strong's Exhaustive Concordance of the Bible, ©1800 Public Domain

[xx] "kolasis," Strongs #2851, Ibid.

[xxi] "*menw*" Strong's #3306, ibid.

[xxii] "*paideuo*" Strong's #3811, ibid.

> **1 Corinthians 11:31-32** For if we would judge ourselves, we should not be judged. But when we are judged, we are chastened (*paideu*) of the Lord, that we should not be condemned with the world. [KJV— the Greek word in parenthesis added by me for clarity.]

In the quote below, the word translated "discipline" is a derivative of the same Greek word *paideuo*, NOT *kolazo* or *kolasis*.

> **Hebrews 12:5-9** And have you forgotten the encouraging words God spoke to you as his children? He said,
>
> > "My child, don't make light of the Lord's discipline, and don't give up when he <u>corrects</u> you. 6 For the Lord <u>disciplines</u> those he loves, and he <u>punishes</u> each one he accepts as his child."
> >
> > 7 As you endure this <u>divine discipline</u>, remember that God is treating you as his own children. Who ever heard of a child who is never <u>disciplined</u> by its father? 8 If God doesn't <u>discipline</u> you as he does all of his children, it means that you are illegitimate and are not really his children at all. 9 **Since we respected our earthly fathers who <u>disciplined</u> us, shouldn't we submit even more to the <u>discipline</u> of the Father of our spirits, and live forever**?—NLT

NONE of the words about the Lord's discipline in this passage (translated "correction," "punishes," and "discipline" in these verses) come from the Greek word *kolazo* used in Jesus' statement about separation and punishment in Matthew 25. ALL of these examples of chastening or disciplining apply to the here and now, *not the hereafter*.

Are we being asked to rethink Hell or rethink *faith*?

Whatever someone uses as their means of "evangelism" (winning the hearts and minds of others to what they believe) is what they've placed front and center. If someone is evangelizing with the threat of Hell, then Hell is front and center as the thing to be feared and avoided. But if those who claim to represent Jesus are saying *belief in Him right now is no longer necessary* and Hell is a temporary "chastisement," how does that put Jesus in the center?

JESUS CHRIST is worthy of all that we are, all that we have, all of our adoration—and He is worthy of it right now. I don't preach on Hell to "win" people to the Lord. And I don't try to evangelize people with descriptions of Heaven. Neither do I try to entice them with "Don't you want to be with your lost loved one—you fill in the blank here with the name of a spouse, child, parent— who is in Heaven?" To do *any* of these is to place something or someone else as the focus of the heart. Of all the things we could use to tell people how to find peace, joy, and Life, there is only ONE—Jesus—that can be the appropriate center of our walk and our words.

It's not so much their ideas about Hell that concern me—rather it's what leaders in Universalism and UR are willing to <u>sacrifice</u> in order to get to the conclusions they have drawn about Hell.

As I said in the beginning of the book, I don't believe that one's opinion on Hell is the determining factor in salvation. But *faith is*. By setting faith in Jesus Christ on the back burner, saying it's not a necessity but an enhancement for life here, Universalists are attempting to redefine Christianity. For me, living for Jesus *today* isn't a perk—it's everything!

In addition, Universalists who promote their views of the New Testament give the world the example of cutting and pasting select passages of the Bible, of minimizing, ignoring, or denying any concepts that might offend the world—including the words and actions of Jesus which call us to faith. It is, in my opinion, an unwise course. Producers at powerful media outlets have used the fuzzy logic of Universalists as fuel for their arguments that Jesus was just a guy who meant well, but died like any other man. They exploit the controversy to market a version of "history" to the world that claims Jesus' words (if He really even said them) were just staged, zealous rhetoric, and that the Bible can mean whatever people want it to mean. . . . So whether or not Universalists were willing partners in secular media's distorted view of Jesus, they have aided in promoting it none-the-less.

If you are going to accept what Universalists say about eternity, you'd better pay attention to how they got to where they are standing and consider if you want to stand there with them.

Is **Hell "redemptive"?** *Will* God give those who rejected Him in this life more chances to accept Him? Is it, as Carlton Pearson and others claim, that "the world is already saved, they just don't know it"?[xxiii] Can "love win" only if everyone is in Heaven?

According to some (including Rob Bell if I understand him correctly), the punishment of Hell only lasts until the person repents, (and then they can be let out of Hell and into Heaven?). According to the Christian Universalist Association, those who died without faith will be given more opportunities when the saints who were resurrected first "preach the gospel" to them.[xxiv]

Certainly, there are still many details about Heaven, judgment, etc. that are not given to any of us. I can say there is A LOT I don't know about what will happen when we die . . . but I'm not going to make something up and *hope* it's true, or worse yet, let the product of my wishful thinking become an offer I make to others in God's name.

In an article entitled *Answers to 21 Anti-universalist Objections*, the question is asked, if justice doesn't demand that some people pay for their sins forever. Steve Jones responds,

> "No. The wages of sin is death — we'll all make that payment."[xxv]

First of all, *we* don't "pay" the wages for sin—Scripture says there is NO payment that *we* can make that would absolve us of sin—we *receive* the wages of our sin (what we earned). Mr. Jones is mostly right, though, when he says that all will die. Unless they are alive at the moment Jesus returns, even Christians will die a "death" in our bodies. But this (physical dying) is not the "death" that should concern people. What should concern them is what happens after that. Please read what follows about "death" and "Hell" before you think no one will be judged for their sin.

The Bible says that ALL (not some) of us have fallen short (Romans 3:23, Romans 5:12), all of us are born captive—and nothing but the blood of Jesus can save us.

> **Romans 8:8-11** Those who are in the realm of the flesh *cannot* please God. 9 You, however, are not in the realm of the flesh but are in the realm of the Spirit, **if** indeed the Spirit of God lives in you. And **if** anyone does not have the Spirit of Christ, they do not belong to Christ.

[xxiii] http://www.beliefnet.com/Faiths/2003/06/*Jesus-Will-Save-You-Whether-You-Agree-Or-Not*.aspx (June 5, 2012)

[xxiv] Two examples are: *Divine Justice and Life After Death* from The Christian Universalist Assoc. website http://www.christianuniversalist.org/articles/justice-afterlife.html and Rob Bell in *Love Wins, A Book About Heaven, Hell, and the Fate of Every Person Who Ever Lived*, (New York HarperCollins Publishers 2011) 109.

[xxv] Internet article, *Answers to 21 Anti-universalist Objections* by Steve Jones http://www.auburn.edu/~allenkc/answers2.html (May 21, 2012)

10 But **if** Christ is in you, then even though your body is subject to death because of sin, the Spirit gives life because of righteousness. 11 And **if** <u>the Spirit of him who raised Jesus from the dead is living in you, he who raised Christ from the dead will also give life to your mortal bodies because of his Spirit who lives in you.</u>

Capitalizing on Common Misunderstandings about Hell and Death (and Hades, Gehenna, and Perdition.)

Technically, neither Jesus nor anyone else in Bible times *ever* actually used the word "Hell." Hell is an Old English/Dutch/German/Indo European catch-all word that has been used by translators to denote several Biblical names for a place people went when they died.

Universalists and those in Universal Reconciliation say they believe <u>everyone</u> will be resurrected and that Hell is temporary (and will be destroyed).

Well . . . in a way, one could say those ideas are Scriptural. Yes. *Really*. But, in the end the answer doesn't mean what most *think* it means. There is more to it than that, and Satan is more than happy to make an endless game out of it. People get so caught up in the game of what if/when/where Hell exists that they don't realize their *guess* is moot! People in Universalism/UR may not be intentionally deceptive about it . . . but Satan is very adept at deception, and he is willing to use *any* misunderstanding to his advantage. It all depends on what is called "compartmentalization"—a big word that means somebody wants to keep handing you bits of information or "facts" to store in separate (compartmentalized) files in your head. They want to be able to draw out ONE partial truth at a time, apply that tidbit to a bigger picture they *claim* is there, then put it back away from view. What's important in this game is that you never open multiple drawers at a time and actually attempt to assemble the pieces, because if you do, you might realize that their "big picture" looks like a jigsaw puzzle where random pieces have been snipped to fit together and pieces of *other* puzzles were substituted to fill in gaps. The result is a nonsensical jumble of colors and lines. But remember, "they" (the teachers/leaders/promoters of these schools of thought) aren't the only participants in the game. It only works if <u>you</u> are a willing participant who doesn't actually *think* about all you are being told. God gave you a rational mind for a purpose. It's up to you to use it.

In UR/Christian Universalism, the string of logic looks like this:

    God loves everyone
+ Everyone is resurrected
<u>+ Hell is temporary and will be destroyed</u>
= Everyone ends up with a "desirable outcome" (Heaven)

So let's look at the elements of the Universal Reconciliation equation and see if they add up to the big picture of everyone in Heaven.

Element #1: Jesus loves everyone.

Yes, I believe He does. He loves people the world calls "good," and the ones they would call "bad" . . . and He loves the disabled, and Buddhists, and mean old men, and soldiers, and selfish people, and lesbians, and babies, and the executives at British Petroleum, and preachers on TBN, and fat people, and Eskimos, and Islamic Terrorists . . . and me.

I'll simply say—absolutely—I do believe that God loves *every*one. For me, God's love isn't in question; it's how people define what that love is and how it works that can muddy our understanding of it. If we each are allowed to define what true "love" is, then the resulting pictures are different.

Do you believe that God's perfect "love" is expressed by *dragging* people against their wills to His solutions? Do you believe that God's love will never bring the promised justice to those to whom it has been denied? Do you believe that God's perfect love doesn't ask for (or allow) a genuine response from us? For Universalists, the answer to all of the above is "yes." Consider well what *you* believe.

Element #2: Every person will eventually be raised from the dead.

I believe it is solidly stated in Scripture.

Here is a *brief* List of New Testament Scriptures that Speak of the Resurrection:

Mark 16 (whole chapter)
Matthew 27:53
Luke 20:35-36
John 5:29
John 11:23-25
Acts 1:22, 2:26, 2:31, 4:2, 4:33, 13:33, 17:18, 17:32, 23:6, 24:15, 24:21
Romans 1:4, 5:10, 6:5
1 Corinthians 15 (whole chapter)
Philippians 3:10-11
Colossians 3:1
1 Thessalonians 4:13
2 Timothy 1:10, 2:18
Hebrews 6:2, 11:35
1 Peter 1:3, 3:21
Revelation 20:5-6

Element #3: Hell is temporary and will be destroyed.

What I want you to know is that when the word "Hell" is applied to Hades, Gehenna, or sometimes to "Perdition," these terms refer to *a holding place* where the unrighteous dead go, *awaiting* final judgment—like being in a local jail before a trial. Certainly not a pleasant place, but just a holding tank, since the final judgment will not happen until the end of time as we know it.

But if you are thinking of Hell (Hades/Gehenna) as the Bible's ultimate and *final* place of punishment, a person who wants you to believe in Universal Reconciliation can say, "No worries! Hell is temporary!" and read this bit of a verse from the last book of the Bible as backup:

Revelation 20:14 "Then death and Hades were thrown into the lake of fire."

Huzzah! And there was great rejoicing! No more death! No more Hell!

But *do* their three elements add up to "everyone ends up in Heaven"?

Let's retrace our final step in the equation before we think the issues with death and Hell are resolved. Element #3 is based on what most people see as (the ultimate) "death" being destroyed. It is also based on the *assumption* that the place most of the NT verses call "Hell" is destroyed as well, leading people to conclude that what remains is the "desirable outcome."

But what comes *before and after* the highly touted verse that says, "Then death and Hades (Hell) were thrown into the lake of fire"? Here's what comes before it:

Revelation 20:4-6 I saw thrones on which were seated those who had been given authority to judge. And I saw the souls of those who had been beheaded because of their testimony about Jesus and because of the word of God. They had not worshiped the beast or its image and had not received its mark on their foreheads or their hands. They came to life and reigned with Christ a thousand years. 5 (The rest of the dead did not come to life until the thousand years were ended.) This is the first resurrection. 6 <u>Blessed and holy are those who share in the first resurrection. The **second death** has no power over *them*</u>, but they will be priests of God and of Christ and will reign with him for a thousand years.—NIV, words in parentheses ( ) are in the actual text, not added by me.

In the verses above, we are told of the "first resurrection" which applies to those who held onto Jesus even unto death. Note the words: "The second death has no power over them." Also note that these people will "reign" with Christ over all the earth (where people are still alive in mortal bodies but will experience the blessed reign of the King of Kings). Satan will be imprisoned for this time of Christ's rule. There are no other "resurrections" mentioned as taking place for a thousand years, when Jesus will sit in Judgment of them.

Revelation 20:7-10 When the thousand years are over, Satan will be released from his prison 8 and will go out to deceive the nations in the four corners of the earth—Gog and Magog—and to gather them for battle. In number they are like the sand on the seashore. 9 They marched across the breadth of the earth and surrounded the camp of God's people, the city he loves. But fire came down from heaven and devoured them. 10 And the devil, who deceived them, was *<u>thrown into the lake of burning sulfur</u>*, where the beast and the false prophet had been thrown. They will be tormented day and night for ever and ever.

Please note the "lake of burning sulfur" in the verses above. Now, in the *next* verses, we see *the rest of the dead* (who were not part of the "first resurrection") are raised from the dead—brought out of Hades (which is "under the earth")—and they are "judged." Then Hades (Hell) and death are thrown into the lake. We are also told the name of the lake. It is called "the second death."

Revelation 20:11-15 Then I saw a great white throne and him who was seated on it. The earth and the heavens fled from his presence, and there was no place for them. 12 And I saw the dead, great and small, standing before the throne, and books were opened. Another book was opened, which is the book of life. The dead were judged according to what they had done as recorded in the books. 13 The sea gave up the dead that were in it, and death and Hades gave up the dead that were in them, and each person was judged according to what they had done. 14 Then death and Hades were thrown into the lake of fire. <u>The lake of fire is the **second death**. 15 Anyone whose name was not found written in the book of life was thrown into the lake of fire.</u>

Wait. There is a *second* death? That's what it says. Whether in the first resurrection or the one 1,000 years later, <u>everyone</u> *is* eventually brought back to life—but some are brought back to everlasting life and some are to be judged and face the lake of fire. Those are not my words, but the words of Scripture. Also note there is a "book" (singular) listed in addition to "books" (plural). The "books" (plural) contain all that we have done—and even if you're a nice guy—good works will never outweigh your sin and get you into Heaven. The only "BOOK" where you definitely want your name written is the "book of life," and if your name is in this book, nothing else matters. Note anyone whose name was NOT found in that book was thrown into the lake of fire. (At the very least, this implies that some names might not be there).

Here is the term "second death" in a declaration by the Holy Spirit:

> **Revelation 2:11** Whoever has ears, let them hear what the Spirit says to the churches. The one who is victorious will not be hurt at all by the <u>second death</u>.

"Oh," someone might say, *"this is all in Revelation and you know how everything is symbolic. Who is to know what it all means?"* Well, I'm not the one who uses the quote, "Then death and Hades were thrown into the lake of fire." (From Revelation 20:14) to prove that Hell is temporary. He who thinks he "lives" via the Revelation quote may find that he actually "dies" via the Revelation quote.

Plus, Jesus says more about this fire—the second death—in Matthew 25 (I'll quote it below).

For whom was the fire made?

According to Jesus, it was made for the devil and his angels.

So, the lake of fire *wasn't* made for *people*?

No, but they aren't excluded. They *can* go there.

> **Matthew 25:34-43** [Jesus speaking] "Then the King will say to those on his right, 'Come, you who are blessed by my Father; take your inheritance, the kingdom prepared for you since the creation of the world. 35 For I was hungry and you gave me something to eat, I was thirsty and you gave me something to drink, I was a stranger and you invited me in, 36 I needed clothes and you clothed me, I was sick and you looked after me, I was in prison and you came to visit me.'
>
> 37 "Then the righteous will answer him, 'Lord, when did we see you hungry and feed you, or thirsty and give you something to drink? 38 When did we see you a stranger and invite you in, or needing clothes and clothe you? 39 When did we see you sick or in prison and go to visit you?'
>
> 40 "The King will reply, 'Truly I tell you, whatever you did for one of the least of these brothers and sisters of mine, you did for me.'
>
> 41 "<u>Then he will say to those on his left, 'Depart from me, you who are cursed, into the eternal fire prepared for the devil and his angels</u>. 42 For I was hungry and you gave me nothing to eat, I was thirsty and you gave me nothing to drink, 43 I was a stranger and you did not invite me in, I needed clothes and you did not clothe me, I was sick and in prison and you did not look after me.' "

THIS is in the same parable of the sheep and the goats that Rob Bell and others use to claim a temporary Hell—yet it speaks of people being sent into the *fire prepared for Satan and his angels*. It is consistent with what Peter the apostle also wrote:

> **2 Peter 2:4-9** For if God did not spare angels when they sinned, but sent them to hell, putting them in chains of darkness to be held for judgment; 5 if he did not spare the ancient world when he brought the flood on its ungodly people, but protected Noah, a preacher of righteousness, and seven others; 6 if he condemned the cities of Sodom and Gomorrah by burning them to ashes, and made them an example of what is going to happen to the ungodly; 7 and if he rescued Lot, a righteous man, who was distressed by the depraved conduct of the lawless 8 (for that righteous man, living among them day after day, was tormented in his righteous soul by the lawless deeds he saw and heard)—9 if this is so, then the Lord knows

how to rescue the godly from trials and to hold the unrighteous for punishment on the day of judgment.

Here is another place where Jesus presented the concept of a resurrection for all (with some rising to life and some to condemnation).

John 5:24-29 [Jesus speaking] "Very truly I tell you, whoever hears my word and believes him who sent me has eternal life and will not be judged but has crossed over from death to life. 25 Very truly I tell you, a time is coming and has now come when the dead will hear the voice of the Son of God and those who hear will live. 26 For as the Father has life in himself, so he has granted the Son also to have life in himself. 27 And he has given him authority to judge because he is the Son of Man.

28 "Do not be amazed at this, for a time is coming when all who are in their graves will hear his voice 29 and come out—those who have done what is good will rise to live, and those who have done what is evil will rise to be condemned."

PLEASE NOTE:

This passage DOES talk about people doing "good" but you need to put this in the light of Jesus words that only those things done in Him (built with Christ as the foundation) are good, only those works we have done in Him will remain.

The word for "condemned" here is NOT *kolazo* (pruning). It is the word *krisis* (*Strong's* #2920) which is defined as : "a separating, sundering, separation, a trial, contest, selection, judgment, opinion or decision given concerning anything, esp. concerning justice and injustice, right or wrong, sentence of condemnation, damnatory judgment, condemnation and punishment . . ."[xxvi]

Jesus used the same concept here when speaking to the religious hypocrites of the day:

Matthew 23:33 "You serpents, you brood of vipers, how will you escape the sentence (*krisis*) of hell (*Gehenna*)?" –NIV [Greek words added by me for clarity]

The notion isn't just dying and being in the grave, but a *judgment* (which isn't until everything is over) and this judgment being connected to what was (in the mindset of the day) the ultimate place of punishment.

Finally, let us read the words of the LORD from the last chapter of the last book of the Bible:

Revelation 21:5-8 He who was seated on the throne said, "I am making everything new!" Then he said, "Write this down, for these words are trustworthy and true."

6 He said to me: "It is done. I am the Alpha and the Omega, the Beginning and the End. To the thirsty I will give water without cost from the spring of the water of life. 7 Those who are victorious will inherit all this, and I will be their God and they will be my children. 8 But the cowardly, the unbelieving, the vile, the murderers, the sexually immoral, those who practice magic arts, the idolaters and all liars—they will be consigned to the fiery lake of burning sulfur. This is the second death."

---

xxvi "Condemnation" James Strong, *Strong's Exhaustive Concordance of the Bible*, ©1800 Public Domain

These aren't *my* words. This is what God says. Do you see any winking on His part? Any hints of rescue of the ousted ones? Anything that plainly points to *temporary* discomfort? I don't. Even if, somehow, this second death was mere annihilation (ceasing to exist)—I wouldn't consider this a "desirable outcome."

More Universalist thoughts on Hell from Steve Jones and Gerry Watts

In response to a verse in Matthew 10:28 ("God is able to destroy both body and soul in hell.") Universalist Steve Jones says that just because "God has the power to do something doesn't mean He does it." Jones then says that Jesus' words were given in a "send-off to his missionaries" (the disciples) who were going out to preach and face opposition. According to Jones, Jesus was merely warning them not to be "consumed by the fear of men, but instead to fear the one who truly holds the power of life and death," so it's not necessarily a statement about Hell.[xxvii]

If this was the only place Jesus ever made that particular statement about Hell, we *might* be able to apply it the way Mr. Jones does. However, in the Gospel of Luke before a crowd of *thousands*, Jesus made the same statement—and the *context* is religious hypocrisy (catering to our own desires or those of others and calling it godly) as opposed to actually living for God. Jesus connects their (our) denial of Him with being disowned in the age to come.

> **Luke 12:3-10** Meanwhile, when a crowd of many thousands had gathered, so that they were trampling on one another, Jesus began to speak first to his disciples, saying: "Be on your guard against the yeast of the Pharisees, which is hypocrisy. 2 There is nothing concealed that will not be disclosed, or hidden that will not be made known. 3 What you have said in the dark will be heard in the daylight, and what you have whispered in the ear in the inner rooms will be proclaimed from the roofs.
>
> 4 "I tell you, my friends, do not be afraid of those who kill the body and after that can do no more. 5 But I will show you whom you should fear: Fear him who, after your body has been killed, has authority to throw you into hell. Yes, I tell you, fear him. 6 Are not five sparrows sold for two pennies? Yet not one of them is forgotten by God. 7 Indeed, the very hairs of your head are all numbered. Don't be afraid; you are worth more than many sparrows.
>
> 8 "I tell you, whoever publicly acknowledges me before others, the Son of Man will also acknowledge before the angels of God. 9 But whoever disowns me before others will be disowned before the angels of God. 10 And everyone who speaks a word against the Son of Man will be forgiven, but anyone who blasphemes against the Holy Spirit <u>will not</u> be forgiven.

In an article written by Gerry Watts entitled, *God is The Saviour of All Mankind - Yet why don't most Christians really believe this?*, he says that there "isn't any mention of 'Hell' or Gehenna in the book of Acts, or Paul's writings, or Peter's writings," and asks, if it is so important why the apostles and the early church didn't present the idea clearly. He posits that it's because it "was not a part of the original gospel of grace." [xxviii]

---

xxvii Internet article, *Answers to 21 Anti-universalist Objections* by Steve Jones http://www.auburn.edu/~allenkc/answers2.html (May 21, 2012)

Only if we allow people to redefine, redact, and misplace Scriptures and other writings about the early church can they assert that "early" Christians had no belief in eternal punishment/judgment.

And, by his argument, Mr. Watts makes it sound as if the words of Jesus Christ in the Gospels of Matthew, Mark, Luke and John are meaningless fluff. If the words of Jesus were not enough to make the point, here are words about everlasting destruction in other books of the New Testament. (I suppose *technically* the word "Hell" isn't here . . . but I'm not playing a game with terms. Read and discern.)

Written by Paul:

> **2 Thessalonians 1:5-10** All this is evidence that God's judgment is right, and as a result you will be counted worthy of the kingdom of God, for which you are suffering. 6 God is just: He will pay back trouble to those who trouble you 7 and give relief to you who are troubled, and to us as well. This will happen when the Lord Jesus is revealed from heaven in blazing fire with his powerful angels. 8 He will punish those who do not know God and do not obey the gospel of our Lord Jesus. 9 <u>They will be punished with everlasting destruction and shut out from the presence of the Lord and from the glory of his might</u> 10 on the day he comes to be glorified in his holy people and to be marveled at among all those who have believed. This includes you, because you believed our testimony to you.

> **Philippians 1:27-28** Only be sure as citizens so to conduct yourselves [that] your manner of life [will be] worthy of the good news (the Gospel) of Christ, so that whether I [do] come and see you or am absent, I may hear this of you: that you are standing firm in united spirit and purpose, striving side by side and contending with a single mind for the faith of the glad tidings (the Gospel). 28And do not [for a moment] be frightened or intimidated in anything by your opponents and adversaries, for such [constancy and fearlessness] will be a clear sign (proof and seal) to them of [their impending] <u>destruction</u>, but [a sure token and evidence] of your deliverance and salvation, and that from God. — [Amplified Bible]

> **Philippians 3:18-19** For there are many, of whom I have often told you and now tell you even with tears, who walk (live) as enemies of the cross of Christ (the Anointed One).
>
> 19 <u>They are doomed and their fate is eternal misery (perdition)</u>; their god is their stomach (their appetites, their sensuality) and they glory in their shame, siding with earthly things and being of their party. — [Amplified Bible]

> **2 Corinthians 2:15-16** Our lives are a Christ-like fragrance rising up to God. But this fragrance is perceived differently by those who are being saved and by those who are perishing. 16 To those who are perishing, we are a dreadful smell of death and doom. But to those who are being saved, we are a life-giving perfume.

Written by Peter the apostle:

> **2 Peter 3:3-9** Above all, you must understand that in the last days scoffers will come, scoffing and following their own evil desires. 4 They will say, "Where is this 'coming' he promised? Ever since our ancestors died, everything goes on as it has since the beginning of creation." 5 But they deliberately forget that long ago by God's word the heavens came into

---

xxviii PDF article on the internet by Gerry Watts, http://purposeoflife.org.uk/files/Download/saviour_of_all_mankind.pdf (May 22, 2012)

being and the earth was formed out of water and by water. 6 By these waters also the world of that time was deluged and destroyed. 7 <u>By the same word the present heavens and earth are reserved for fire, being kept for the day of judgment and destruction of the ungodly.</u> 8 But do not forget this one thing, dear friends: With the Lord a day is like a thousand years, and a thousand years are like a day. 9 The Lord is not slow in keeping his promise, as some understand slowness. Instead he is patient with you, not wanting anyone to perish, but everyone to come to repentance.

From the book of Jude (who was a brother of Jesus Christ):

Jude 1:3-7 Dear friends, although I was very eager to write to you about the salvation we share, I felt compelled to write and urge you to contend for the faith that was once for all entrusted to God's holy people. 4 <u>For certain individuals whose condemnation was written about long ago</u> have secretly slipped in among you. They are ungodly people, who pervert the grace of our God into a license for immorality and deny Jesus Christ our only Sovereign and Lord.

5 Though you already know all this, I want to remind you that the Lord at one time delivered his people out of Egypt, but later destroyed those who did not believe. 6 <u>And the angels who did not keep their positions of authority but abandoned their proper dwelling—these he has kept in darkness, bound with everlasting chains for judgment on the great Day.</u> 7 In a similar way, Sodom and Gomorrah and the surrounding towns gave themselves up to sexual immorality and perversion. <u>They serve as an example of those who suffer the punishment of eternal fire.</u>

From the book of Hebrews in the New Testament:

Hebrews 6:1-2 Therefore let us go on and get past the elementary stage in the teachings and doctrine of Christ (the Messiah), advancing steadily toward the completeness and perfection that belong to spiritual maturity. Let us not again be laying the foundation of repentance and abandonment of dead works (dead formalism) and of the faith [by which you turned] to God, with teachings about purifying, the laying on of hands, <u>the resurrection from the dead, and eternal judgment and punishment.</u> [These are all matters of which you should have been fully aware long, long ago.] — Amplified Bible

When Jesus first sent out His disciples, He told them that if their message was rejected where they went, they were to shake the dust off of their feet as a witness against that town on the Day of Judgment.

Matthew 10:14-15 "If anyone will not welcome you or listen to your words, leave that home or town and shake the dust off your feet. Truly I tell you, it will be more bearable for Sodom and Gomorrah on the day of judgment than for that town."

Mark 6:11 "And if any place will not welcome you or listen to you, leave that place and shake the dust off your feet as a testimony against them."

Luke 9:5 "If people do not welcome you, leave their town and shake the dust off your feet as a testimony against them."

From the book of Acts:

When Paul the apostle and Barnabas were traveling in Pisidian of Antioch they were rejected by the Jewish leaders and so they "shook the dust off their feet as a warning to them."

Acts 13:49-51 The word of the Lord spread through the whole region. 50 But the Jewish leaders incited the God-fearing women of high standing and the leading men of the city. They stirred up persecution against Paul and Barnabas, and expelled them from their region. 51 So they shook the dust off their feet as a warning to them and went to Iconium.

Here are other Scriptures that speak of the wrath of God—in reference to those who have faith in Jesus and those who don't.

John 9:36 [Jesus speaking] Whoever believes in the Son has eternal life, but whoever rejects the Son will not see life, for God's wrath remains on them.[xxix]

Romans 2:4-9 Or do you show contempt for the riches of his kindness, forbearance and patience, not realizing that God's kindness is intended to lead you to repentance? 5 But because of your stubbornness and your unrepentant heart, you are storing up wrath against yourself for the day of God's wrath, when his righteous judgment will be revealed. 6 God "will repay each person according to what they have done." 7 To those who by persistence in doing good seek glory, honor and immortality, he will give eternal life. 8 But for those who are self-seeking and who reject the truth and follow evil, there will be wrath and anger.

Verse 6 refers to Psalm 62:12 and Prov. 24:12

Romans 5:9 "Since we have now been justified by his blood, how much more shall we be saved from God's wrath through him!"

The "we" in context is Paul and the ones to whom he was writing: the Church (believers) in Rome. Keep in mind that those who belong to Jesus are promised to be saved from God's wrath.

1 Thessalonians 1:7-10 And so you became a model to all the believers in Macedonia and Achaia. 8 The Lord's message rang out from you not only in Macedonia and Achaia—your faith in God has become known everywhere. Therefore we do not need to say anything about it, 9 for they themselves report what kind of reception you gave us. They tell how you turned to God from idols to serve the living and true God, 10 and to wait for his Son from heaven, whom he raised from the dead—Jesus, who rescues us from the coming wrath.

1 Thessalonians 5:4-9 But you, brothers and sisters, are not in darkness so that this day should surprise you like a thief. 5 You are all children of the light and children of the day. We do not belong to the night or to the darkness. 6 So then, let us not be like others, who are asleep, but let us be awake and sober. 7 For those who sleep, sleep at night, and those who get drunk, get drunk at night. 8 But since we belong to the day, let us be sober, putting on faith and love as a breastplate, and the hope of salvation as a helmet. 9 For God did not appoint us to suffer wrath but to receive salvation through our Lord Jesus Christ.

Hebrews 3:10-12 [the Lord being quoted] And so I was provoked (displeased and sorely grieved) with that generation, and said, They always err and are led astray in their hearts, and they have not perceived or recognized My ways and become progressively better and more experimentally and intimately acquainted with them.

11 Accordingly, I swore in My wrath and indignation, They shall not enter into My rest.

[xxix] The word translated "remains" here is the Greek word "meno" which means "held or kept coninually." Strong's #3306, James Strong, Strong's Exhaustive Concordance of the Bible, ©1800 Public Domain

12 [Therefore beware] brethren, take care, lest there be in any one of you a wicked, unbelieving heart [which refuses to cleave to, trust in, and rely on Him], leading you to turn away and desert or stand aloof from the living God.—Amplified Bible

Hebrews 4:2-4 For indeed we have had the glad tidings [Gospel of God] proclaimed to us just as truly as they [the Israelites of old did when the good news of deliverance from bondage came to them]; but the message they heard did not benefit them, because it was not mixed with faith (with the leaning of the entire personality on God in absolute trust and confidence in His power, wisdom, and goodness) by those who heard it; neither were they united in faith with the ones [Joshua and Caleb] who heard (did believe).

3 For we who have believed (adhered to and trusted in and relied on God) do enter that rest, in accordance with His declaration that those [who did not believe] should not enter when He said, As I swore in My wrath, They shall not enter My rest; and this He said although [His] works had been completed and prepared [and waiting for all who would believe] from the foundation of the world.—Amplified Bible

Hebrews 10:24-27 And let us consider how we may spur one another on toward love and good deeds, 25 not giving up meeting together, as some are in the habit of doing, but encouraging one another—and all the more as you see the Day approaching.

26 If we deliberately keep on sinning after we have received the knowledge of the truth, no sacrifice for sins is left, 27 but only a fearful expectation of judgment and of raging fire that will consume the enemies of God.

Revelation 6:15-17 Then the kings of the earth, the princes, the generals, the rich, the mighty, and everyone else, both slave and free, hid in caves and among the rocks of the mountains. 16 They called to the mountains and the rocks, "Fall on us and hide us from the face of him who sits on the throne and from the wrath of the Lamb! 17 For the great day of their wrath has come, and who can withstand it?"

Revelation 11:18 The nations were angry, and your wrath has come. The time has come for judging the dead, and for rewarding your servants the prophets and your people who revere your name, both great and small— and for destroying those who destroy the earth."

Revelation 14:9-11 A third angel followed them and said in a loud voice: "If anyone worships the beast and its image and receives its mark on their forehead or on their hand, 10 they, too, will drink the wine of God's fury, which has been poured full strength into the cup of his wrath. They will be tormented with burning sulfur in the presence of the holy angels and of the Lamb. 11 And the smoke of their torment will rise for ever and ever. There will be no rest day or night for those who worship the beast and its image, or for anyone who receives the mark of its name."

CHAPTER 6—When Are Words . . . Just Words?

>Jesus said, "Therefore everyone who hears these words of mine and puts them into practice is like a wise man who built his house on the rock. The rain came down, the streams rose, and the winds blew and beat against that house; yet it did not fall, because it had its foundation on the rock. But everyone who hears these words of mine and does not put them into practice is like a foolish man who built his house on sand. The rain came down, the streams rose, and the winds blew and beat against that house, and it fell with a great crash." [Luke 7:24-27]

>Paul the apostle said, "By the grace God has given me, I laid a foundation as a wise builder, and someone else is building on it. But each one should build with care. For no one can lay any foundation other than the one already laid, which is Jesus Christ." [1 Cor. 3:10-11]

Must we always take Scripture at face value?

A lot of debate over Scripture revolves around how each person "sees" it. Some see most of the Bible as law that must be taken literally from start to finish. Others see it as "narrative" (as in a descriptive story) that has meaning but isn't meant to be taken literally. I saw recently that one man was describing the Bible as "a library of books," implying that it was merely a collection of writings.

If we take the whole Bible as "law" (a prescription), then we can justify multiple wives (the kings of the Old Testament had them), consulting mediums (King Saul did), handling poisonous snakes as a testimony to our faith (see Mark 16:18), and many other things that run counter to God's wisdom. Simply because someone can find a verse that *describes* these things in a record of events does not necessarily mean they had the approval of God or are His prescription for those activities. Cults are often formed as people decide to take the record of what someone in the Bible did or said or a direction God gave for a specific place and time—and make it a *template* or law for the practice of faith.

On the other hand, if we read the whole Bible simply as a narrative of stories and events from various perspectives, or just hand-me-down stories with general wisdom in them, then we can pick and choose what "truth" in it suits us. The problem with this is that carefully selected truths sliced from the pages of Scripture can be quoted, but may come at the expense of God's *intended* message.

However, if you take the time to look, you will see that some of the Bible IS law (also called "prescriptive"), some of it IS narrative—a record of what people did (sometimes despite God's leading). Some Scripture is a record of what God did and said to specific people for a specific reason in a specific time and culture. Other passages are what He is saying to all people for all time. Some Scripture is poetry, some of it is proverbs (wise sayings), some of it is allegory or parable. **And, in most cases, merely reading the context tells you which category a specific passage belongs to—but ALL of it is given to us by God and the respect you have for the Bible will often be in direct proportion to the power it brings to your life.**

Yellow Alert! Aye, Captain, there be danger ahead when:

1. A teacher is redefining a word, phrase, or parable in a way that contradicts the *obvious* meaning of it. The Lord *did* use parables, but *didn't* contradict Himself. <u>Jesus wasn't saying one thing in public (with a wink wink, nudge nudge), and then denying it all behind the scenes when He talked to the disciples.</u> The "deeper" meaning of the parable wasn't a contradiction of the obvious meaning. God is not the author of confusion.

2. The concept stated by the teacher can be *read into* passages but it's not directly stated anywhere. In other words, you have to have the teacher's (missing from Scripture) idea supplied to you in order to "see" their revelation.

3. The "proof" verses of the teaching directly contradict a larger number of other Scriptures.

4. They require you to take some words in a passage (that could be used to promote their idea) literally, yet also state that other words in the same passage (that negate their idea) can only be spiritual or symbolic.

Reflection and discussion on the whole of scripture means that—along with what He *has* done and what He *has* promised us, we would see some of what God *hasn't* done and *hasn't* promised us. This means *each of us* will, at times, have to trust Him to hold us up as we walk through the death of some of our false assumptions or wishful thinking.

Nailing Gelatin to the Wall . . .

> "It depends on what the meaning of '*is*' is."—*President Bill Clinton, at his impeachment trial in 1998*

You name any word, sentence, or phrase—and there is *someone* out there who is willing to massage and maneuver it to make it mean something else or to strip it of meaning altogether. Does this mean that language is useless? Does it mean that no one can truly express their intent and have it understood? While language and our capacity to frame it are limited, I think *integrity* goes a long way toward allowing the words of others to retain true meaning. Before someone takes offense that I used the word "integrity" here, let me define it as the Oxford Dictionary (and I) define it:

1. the state of being whole and undivided
2. the condition of being unified or sound in construction
3. internal consistency . . . [xxx]

I read years ago that integrity is like the thread that goes all the way through the cloth, completely woven INTO the cloth, helping to hold it together. And THIS is what I mean about integrity. Look for ideas and concepts that God has woven throughout His word.

There will always be people who either intentionally or unintentionally detour the meaning of even the most sacred things . . . but if we all keep our eyes on Jesus (the Truth) He can and will liberate true meaning for us—give integrity to what is expressed.

On the whole, Christians need to stop making "topical" studies their only diet when it comes to the Bible. Certainly God offers us wisdom on weight loss and happy marriages and true prosperity, but <u>when we skip over everything</u> else to get to that one nugget in each book of the Bible that

---

[xxx] "integrity" http://oxforddictionaries.com/definition/english/integrity?q=integrity (August 24, 2012)

supports the latest teaching, we're missing so much more. We've developed this sort of "Google it" mentality with the Bible, thinking that's as good as *knowing* it, and in so doing *we* are setting ourselves up for those who will lift verses out of context and use alternate definitions to mold our understanding around the latest pop theology. When we passively allow others to think *for* us WE abdicate our responsibility in personally knowing and walking with God. Let me give some examples:

> **John 14:6 [Jesus speaking]** "I am the way and the truth and the life. No one comes to the Father except through me."

In his book *Love Wins*, after quoting the above verse, Rob Bell claims that Jesus doesn't say *how* people will get to God through Him. According to Bell, Jesus is simply saying that whatever the Lord may doing, it's somehow being done through Him. [xxxi]

Yet, when I read the Bible, even within the Gospel of John, I see Jesus repeatedly declaring that people must come to God through *faith* in Him. (John 3:16-18, John 5:24-30, John 6:39-40, John 8:12, John 15:5-6 & 8, John 17:1-3) If we included the other Gospels, there would be MANY explicit statements made by Jesus about *how* people come to the Father (eternal life). Let me just quote Jesus' words in **John 5:24** here:

> "Very truly I tell you, whoever hears my word and believes him who sent me has eternal life and will not be judged but has crossed over from death to life."

I cannot comprehend how (or *why*) Mr. Bell thinks that Jesus was ambiguous about salvation . . . unless he believes all Jesus' statements in all four gospels on the topic of salvation are somehow mistaken.

The words of Gerry Beauchemin

Another proponent of Universal Reconciliation, Gerry Beauchemin, posted an article entitled *Is This Universalism?* [xxxii] as a sort of prelude to a book he wrote on Universalism. (Mr. Beauchemin, I'm told, is considered an authority or spokesperson for some in the Universal Reconciliation movement.) He uses a few paragraphs in the beginning of his article to say that Universal Reconciliation (which he calls "*Christian* Universalism") is different from the world's (version of) Universalism because those in Christian Universalism believe that Jesus is the one through whom all are reconciled, whereas the world's version of Universalism merely says all beliefs are the same. [And, again, I am not addressing what he calls the "Universalism of the world" in this book.]

Mr. Beauchemin lists John 3:16, as proof that God loves everyone and says that 1 John 2:2 shows us the blood of Jesus "propitiates the sins of the whole world." He goes on to say that the blood of Jesus is a "universal propitiation," and that eventually "every knee will bow in sincere worship of Jesus Christ" which he defines as "universal worship." [xxxiii]

Let's address these ideas.

[xxxi] Rob Bell, *Love Wins, A Book About Heaven, Hell, and the Fate of Every Person Who Ever Lived*, (New York HarperCollins Publishers 2011) 154.

[xxxii] *Is this Universalism?* by Gerry Beauchemin, posted on April 27, 2011, http://www.hopebeyondhell.net/is-this-universalism-2/ accessed on March 29, 2012

[xxxiii] Ibid.

In John 3:16, all the English versions of the Bible I know of say that God *loves* "the world." BUT then they also say, "that *whosoever believes* in Him shall not perish . . ." That's a *conditional* statement made by Jesus Christ. Jesus then goes on to say in John 3:18:

> "He who believes in Him [who clings to, trusts in, relies on Him] is not judged [he who trusts in Him never comes up for judgment; for him there is no rejection, no condemnation—he incurs no damnation]; but he who does not believe (cleave to, rely on, trust in Him) is judged already [he has already been convicted and has already received his sentence] because he has not believed in and trusted in the name of the only begotten Son of God. [He is condemned for refusing to let his trust rest in Christ's name.]"—Amplified Bible

This does not fit with Universalism's claim of no condemnation for any person.

The second Bible passage Mr. Beauchemin listed (1 John 2:2) *does* say,

> "He is the atoning sacrifice for our sins, and not only for ours but also for the sins of the whole world."

Yep. It says that. I don't in any way dispute that Jesus died for the sins of the whole world. Jesus Himself said it. It's a gift He *offers* to the whole world . . . and like any gift you must *choose* to receive it. Paul the apostle said:

> **Titus 2:11-14** "God's readiness to give and forgive is now public. Salvation's <u>available</u> for everyone! We're being shown how to turn our backs on a godless, indulgent life, and how to take on a God-filled, God-honoring life. This new life is starting right now, and is whetting our appetites for the glorious day when our great God and Savior, Jesus Christ, appears. He *offered himself* as a sacrifice to free us from a dark, rebellious life into this good, pure life, making us a people he can be proud of, energetic in goodness.—*The Message*

In building his case for all being reconciled, Mr. Beauchemin goes on to say that God has both the power and the will to save all people [xxxiv] and lists 1 Tim. 2:3-4—presumably as a scripture that he believes states this.

Here is what **1 Timothy 2:3-4** actually says:

> This is good, and pleases God our Savior, who wants all people to be saved and to come to a knowledge of the truth.

I agree that God *wants* all people to be saved (but I don't come to the same conclusion as Mr. Beauchemin who sees God forbidding freewill in humanity).

Gerry then says that God loves everyone and no one is excluded.[xxxv] Okay. I have no problem with that. I agree God loves every person. We are all created in His image and none is excluded from His love.

As the crown of his idea, Mr. Beauchemin then says that every knee will bow in "sincere worship"[xxxvi] with the idea that, if everyone is "bowing" at the end that means everyone is saved.

[xxxiv] Is this Universalism? by Gerry Beauchemin, posted on April 27, 2011, http://www.hopebeyondhell.net/is-this-universalism-2/ accessed on March 29, 2012.

[xxxv] Ibid

[xxxvi] Ibid.

This is an idea I've seen in *all* the Christian Universalist and Universal Reconciliation material I can ever remember reading. The first four words, "every knee will (or shall) bow" are a piece of a verse in Philippians (2:10), but what about the second half of the idea that says it will be in "sincere worship"? That isn't in the verse (or anywhere that I know of).

Let's go ahead give a quick look at the scene depicted:

> **Philippians 2:9-11** Therefore God exalted him to the highest place and gave him the name that is above every name, 10 **that at the name of Jesus every knee should bow, in heaven and on earth and *under* the earth,** 11 and every tongue acknowledge that Jesus Christ is Lord, to the glory of God the Father.

Who is bowing?
1. The faithful who have died and are present with Him in Heaven
2. *Everyone else*
    a. Those who have died who *aren't* in Heaven—who, at the time they are bowing, are "under the earth" in the place called "Hell," Gehenna, Sheol.
    b. Others who are still ON earth who are still alive (and I would suggest that these may be those who have come through the thousand year reign, at the end of all things)

My question is: WHEN and HOW did/do these people become *believers*? Scripture states that when believers die, they are with the Lord, not "under the earth" (in Hell). Those who belong to Jesus will not be judged but have passed from death to life. (2 Corinthians 5:4-8, John 5:24)

But, according to Universalism and UR, for those who were "under" and on the earth, the act of bowing somehow demonstrates they are all saved and will be allowed entrance to Heaven.

The first problem with this line of thinking: According to the Bible, we are saved (made righteous) by *faith*, not by works (such as bowing)—and not by paying for our sin via a season in Hell/Purgatory. To bow after the Earth's clock has stopped is no longer an act of "faith." To bow simply because you were punished isn't an act of worship *or* faith. Rather, to bow when Jesus Christ is standing before you in all His splendor is a recognition of what can *no longer be denied*.

> **Hebrews 11:1-2** <u>Faith is the confidence</u> that what we hope for will actually happen; it gives us assurance <u>about things we cannot see</u>. 2 Through their faith, the people in days of old earned a good reputation.

The 11th chapter of Hebrews then goes on to list a host of men and women who lived and died before the time of Christ, who *by faith* were counted righteous and says of them:

> **Hebrews 11:13-16** All these people died still *believing what God had promised them.* They did not receive what was promised, but they saw it all from a distance and welcomed it. They agreed that they were foreigners and nomads here on earth. 14 Obviously people who say such things are looking forward to a country they can call their own. 15 If they had longed for the country they came from, they could have gone back. 16 But they were looking for a better place, a heavenly homeland. That is why God is not ashamed to be called their God, for he has prepared a city for them.

"Faith" is defined in this passage by saying that these people all walked in THIS life—here on earth—believing God's promise when they *couldn't* see it. When we are dead, it will no longer be "by faith" that we believe God—we will see Him.

Here is the same concept in Paul's letters to the Corinthians:

> **2 Corinthians 4:18** So we fix our eyes not on what is seen, but on what is unseen, since what is seen is temporary, but what is unseen is eternal.

> **2 Corinthians 5:7** For we live by believing and not by seeing.—NLT

And in the book of Romans:

> **Romans 8:24** For in [this] hope we were saved. But hope [the object of] which is seen is not hope. For how can one hope for what he already sees?—AMP

Second Problem: Mr. Beauchemin and many other Universalists use the "every knee will bow" quote from Philippians because they are moving in the *assumption* that only those who are *happy* to bow do so. I submit that those who are defeated in battle must bow to the one who conquers them—but it isn't in jubilation. Those who are found guilty in court *must* honor and respect (bow to the wishes of) the judge who has found them guilty, but it isn't with joy. Please note that the Amplified Bible, in footnotes to Philippians 2:10 says, the word that is translated in various English versions as "shall" or "will" (in reference to the *bowing*) implies something that will be done under "authority or *compulsion*."[xxxvii]

Third Problem: We should also note that when everyone is seen bowing in this passage, the final judgment has *not yet* taken place. It isn't as if this is the last view of Heaven and now the endless party is going to start. If it was, there would be no more people "under" the earth. The scene here is the return of Jesus Christ when "every eye" shall see him. The final judgment is *yet* to come.

Food for thought: We are told that Adam and Eve were expelled from the garden because God didn't want them to eat of the tree of life (living eternally in their sinful state), no longer able to walk in open relationship with Him.

Please note, Adam and Eve were already *aware* of their sin (they were ashamed and hid from God), so it wasn't just a recognition that something was wrong that would turn it around.

The Lord's solution didn't involve giving Adam and Eve a big "chastising" and then a do-over *within* the Garden. The question isn't whether or not God *could* have somehow solved the problem while they were still in paradise. He is the Almighty. So the question we need to ask ourselves is: If the Lord chose to oust them and limit all of humanity to this physical plane, then declare that we are restored to Him by *faith* (by trusting God in what we cannot see), what makes Universalists think that some people will get another opportunity *after* this plane of existence when they no longer inhabit bodies?

WHAT IF *this life* is our season of testing and chastisement?

Moving on to some of Mr. Beauchemin's other statements.

At least in Mr. Beauchemin's writings, he does qualify his statements, saying all roads won't take people to God . . . but then he says Jesus looks for lost sheep "no matter where they are" because Jesus "isn't satisfied with ninety-nine out of one hundred" and cites Luke. 15:4.[xxxviii]

[xxxvii] "shall" in footnotes for Philippians 2:10 of *The Amplified Bible*, Copyright © 1958, 1987 by the Zondervan Corporation, The Lockman Foundation. (www.Lockman.org) p 1794

[xxxviii] *Is this Universalism?* by Gerry Beauchemin, posted on April 27, 2011, http://www.hopebeyondhell.net/is-this-universalism-2/ accessed on March 29, 2012

What I want to ask is . . . even within the metaphor of the shepherd and the lost sheep, did the shepherd go after all the sheep on the planet? No. Does this story state or imply that there were no other sheep in the world but the ninety-nine and the one the shepherd searched for? No. All 100 sheep were *his own* sheep and he went for the one that he lost out of HIS herd. I would think that this metaphor refers more to backslidden believers rather than those who have never believed. Jesus DID say that he had another fold (of Gentiles) of whom the Jews were not yet aware . . . but even the word "fold" (as in a set apart group) implies there are ones who are NOT part of the group. Every metaphor or parable has its limitations, and as far as this one is concerned, I think stretching it to say the whole world is what Jesus intended in the metaphor is beyond its limitations. Even the number "100" doesn't appear to have any Biblical significance (such as the numbers 12 or 144 might). NOTE: GOATS (those whom Jesus says He will separate from the sheep at the judgment seat) aren't part of the parable.

WHAT IF...

Okay, so even if we were to ignore that Jesus doesn't mention "goats," let's give Mr., Beauchemin's idea that every person in the whole world constitutes the sheepfold some consideration.

If the whole world is the sheepfold to which Jesus referred and He is seeking the lost one(s), then *how* is He doing that? Aren't WE supposed to be following the One who came to "seek and save the lost,"? Aren't we supposed to be doing what He does? Aren't WE now His hands, His feet, His body? Aren't WE called to be willing to lay down life for the sheep? Or are we "hirelings" who are only in it for what we get out of it, who will flee at the first sign of danger? If you think about it, the parable is predicated on the idea that someone IS indeed "lost," needs to be *sought*, and *brought into* the fold.

In Luke 15, there are in fact three parables about something "lost." A lost sheep, a lost coin, and a lost son. In all three, that which was "lost" (sheep, coin, and son) previously *belonged* to the one who received it back. In the case of the son (the "prodigal son") who was lost, did the father in the story go and track down his son and bring him home? No. It was the young man himself who came to a realization that he had sinned against his father, and set his course for home before he was "found."

While I do believe that Jesus gives an open offer to all—the above parables don't necessarily speak about that.

Mr. Beauchemin also lists a series of scriptures which he believes demonstrate that all people will eventually be saved. I will give you some of them (each of which he displayed with a single, stand-alone statement), then I will give you the context of that verse and any rebuttal.

He lists "Job 23:13" and says, "What He desires He does."[xxxix]

In point of fact, the thought expressed above isn't the whole verse. It's the *second half* of the verse and it took me a while to find the version of the Bible where Mr. Beauchemin got it. It's from the version called the *Common English Bible* (CEB). Regardless of the version, in this passage, Job is bitterly complaining about what God has done to him personally. In essence, what Job is saying here is "God is persecuting me and there is no stopping Him!" Please read the following passage for yourself:

---

xxxix Is this Universalism? by Gerry Beauchemin, posted on April 27, 2011, http://www.hopebeyondhell.net/is-this-universalism-2/ accessed on March 29, 2012

Job 23:13-17 He is of one mind; who can reverse it? What he desires, he does.
14 He carries out what is decreed for me and can do many similar things with me.
15 Therefore, I am scared by his presence; I think and become afraid of him.
16 God has weakened my mind; the Almighty has frightened me.
17 Still I'm not annihilated by darkness; he has hidden deep darkness from me.

This is not a passage in which Job truly honors God's power/decision to save all humanity, but the rant of a man who had lost everything dear to him and was understandably upset.

The next reference Mr. Beauchemin lists is Job 42:2 with the statement that God "can do everything and no purpose of His can be thwarted."[xl]

This is also from the story of Job and it's in the last chapter of the book of Job, but I hope you'll permit me to back up just a bit in Job's story. ***In context***, remember Job bitterly complained about God. The thrust of Job's rant in Chapter 23 was to say God was unfair, that God targeted him with unwarranted punishment . . . to which God responds in Chapter 38 that ***no person*** (including Job) has the right to determine what is fair or just!

Job 38:1-2 Then the LORD spoke to Job out of the storm. He said: 2 "Who is this that obscures my plans with words without knowledge?"

God is angry at Job for obscuring (darkening) His words without knowledge. Then God spends two chapters responding to Job. He describes the vastness of His creation and His wisdom—and wants to know who Job thinks he is to be calling God into question. Here's what comes next.

Job 40:1,2 & 8 The LORD said to Job: "Will the one who contends with the Almighty correct him? . . . Would you *discredit* my justice?"

Job is then sorry for his remarks and realizes he spoke out of emotion, not wisdom. After all of this, Job again speaks (in Job 42). I will put Mr. Beauchemin's selected verse in italics:

Job 42:1-6 Then Job replied to the LORD:
2 *"I know that you can do all things; no purpose of yours can be thwarted.*
3 You asked, 'Who is this that obscures my plans without knowledge?' Surely I spoke of things I did not understand, things too wonderful for me to know.
4 "You said, 'Listen now, and I will speak; I will question you, and you shall answer me.'
5 My ears had heard of you but now my eyes have seen you.
6 Therefore I despise myself and repent in dust and ashes."

Neither Job nor God states that the Lord's "plan" is for all to be saved and no one can stop Him. The Lord says He is God and that we have no right to twist His words, His intentions, or His judgments! We have no right to correct Him or *discredit* His justice! The book of Job is about God being God and humanity not being able to completely discern His ways.

---

xl Is this Universalism? by Gerry Beauchemin, posted on April 27, 2011, http://www.hopebeyondhell.net/is-this-universalism-2/ accessed on March 29, 2012

Will Jesus "drag" all people into heaven?

There are MANY scriptures quoted and ideas put forth in Mr. Beauchemin's article on Universal Reconciliation (web address located in footnote) [xli] But let me address just one more—and I must reiterate here that their approach to "proving" their ideas in the Bible is the place where I have the biggest disappointment with those who teach Universalism and UR.

Here is another stand-alone statement from Mr. Beauchemin:

"Christ draws (drags) all to Himself, not merely 1% of humanity. John 12:32" [xlii]

Nowhere in the entire Bible does it say merely 1% of humanity is going to be saved, nor have I ever heard anyone preach that only 1% will be saved, nor have I ever heard anyone *interpret* anything from the Bible stating such a number *or any other percentage*. I realize it was probably dramatic exaggeration on the part of Mr. Beauchemin, but it's a gross exaggeration that bears no resemblance to anything I've ever been taught or read as a Christian. In chapter 7 of the book of Revelation, it states that the number of people standing before the throne is a number which is so great *no man* can count them! And those people are only the ones who have come out of the great tribulation! No human has any proof, or even any idea of how many people will actually be in Heaven.

But let's look at the two concepts Mr. Beauchemin and other Universalists place in John 12:32. One is the idea that *ALL* will come to Christ. The other is that Jesus will "drag" them all there. Let me start off by quoting this verse from several versions of the Bible.

"And I, when I am lifted up from the earth, will *draw* all people to myself."—NIV

"and I, if I may be lifted up from the earth, will draw all men unto myself." –Young's Literal Translation

"And I, if and when I am lifted up from the earth [on the cross], will draw and attract all men [Gentiles as well as Jews] to Myself."—Amplified Bible

If the verse above is all you see, it might seem to confirm Jesus drawing <u>all</u> people to Heaven. But to make the statement seem even stronger, Mr. B and many other Universalists place the word "drag" next to the word "draw" in brackets or parentheses. (Just so you know, I'm not aware of any English version of the Bible that gives the word "drag" in the text, with or without brackets or parentheses.)

In the interest of giving their idea some thought, though, let's look at it. First of all, YES, "drag" IS a possible variant of the word translated "draw" In this passage. (That could shake the dust off of a traditional Christian's heart, couldn't it?) But please hold on while we explore a bit more about this verse and what it might *really* be saying.

We need to know who Jesus was talking to, what they were talking about, etc. Let's check that out. In the surrounding text, Jesus was talking to the disciples about going to the cross.

John 12:32-33 "And I, when I am lifted up from the earth, will draw all people to myself." <u>He said this to show the kind of death he was going to die.</u>

---

xli Is this Universalism? by Gerry Beauchemin, posted on April 27, 2011, http://www.hopebeyondhell.net/is-this-universalism-2/ accessed on March 29, 2012

xlii Ibid.

Right there it says, "He said this to show *the kind of death* he was going to die." So while it does talk of salvation, in this instance the statement is more about His *manner of death* than anything else. But is there more to it than that? Yes! Jesus made this *same* statement about being "lifted up" in death and "drawing" all people to Himself earlier in the Gospel of John—and in this first reference to being lifted up, He connects His death to salvation through faith in God's provision (not a blanket of salvation thrown over all people). In addition, Jesus ties His death on the cross to a symbol in the Old Testament which reflects the same premise of *faith* in God's provision. Let me show you what I'm talking about. In John 3, Jesus mentions His death in a conversation with a man named Nicodemus:

> **John 3:14-18** [Jesus speaking] "Just as Moses lifted up the snake in the wilderness, so the Son of Man must be lifted up, 15 that *everyone who believes* may have eternal life in him."
>
> 16 "For God so loved the world that he gave his one and only Son, that *whoever believes* in him shall not perish but have eternal life. 17 For God did not send his Son into the world to condemn the world, but to save the world through him. 18 Whoever believes in him is not condemned, but *whoever does not believe* stands condemned already because they *have not believed* in the name of God's one and only Son.

Clearly, there is some option to "not believe" because Jesus says it there—*twice*. It's something Jesus is OFFERING to ALL, but only those who *believe* get what is offered. Am I sure that's what He was saying? Let's look at the Old Testament account Jesus mentions:

> **Numbers 21:6-9** Then the LORD sent venomous snakes among them; they bit the people and many Israelites died. 7 The people came to Moses and said, "We sinned when we spoke against the LORD and against you. Pray that the LORD will take the snakes away from us." So Moses prayed for the people.
>
> 8 The LORD said to Moses, "Make a snake and put it up on a pole; anyone who is bitten can look at it and live." 9 So Moses made a bronze snake and put it up on a pole. Then when anyone was bitten by a snake and looked at the bronze snake, they lived.

Note: In the account of Moses, we see a penalty for sin and God's provision which was available to ALL of them, but EACH of them had to look up at the bronze snake on the pole (believe in God's provision) in order to live. *Jesus* compares this to Himself on the cross.

Now let's deal with the word "drag." Remember, Mr. Beauchemin offered the belief (along with many other teachers of UR) that the intent of Jesus in John 12:32-33 was to say he would "drag" all people to Himself—and I admitted that "drag" is in the list of *possible* meanings for this word. But in light of the bigger context of seeing the mention of the exact same thing (being lifted up on the cross) in John 3—and Jesus comparing this to the provision God made in Numbers 21—I see no language that implies that people will be "dragged" to Christ. In fact, right there in His very discourse about it, Jesus says those who believe are saved, but those who don't believe are condemned already. Not my words, but the words of Jesus.

NOW THINK ABOUT IT:

The word "drag" speaks of force, of *being pulled against your will* to something.

The word "draw" speaks of something gentler, of *attraction to* something, of an *appeal for* something being *offered*.

Jesus' *Actions* Speak as Loud as His Words

Over and over again, Jesus made it clear that it was not just people's words but their deeds that declared where their hearts were. So do the actions of Jesus reveal that He is one who would drag unwilling people into His kingdom? Let's look at just a few examples:

In the Gospels of Matthew and Luke, an account is given of Jesus being led by the Spirit of God to the wilderness. After forty days and nights of fasting, He was hungry. The devil tempted Him by saying, "If you are the Son of God, turn these stones into bread." Jesus refused. Why? He came to live a life as a man submitted to (and dependent upon) God. He would not use the power He had to provide for Himself.

The devil then tempted Him by taking Him to the highest point of the temple (about 180 feet up) and said, "If you are the Son of God, throw yourself down. For it is written: 'He will command his angels concerning you, and they will lift you up in their hands, so that you will not strike your foot against a stone.'" But Jesus refused. Why? Didn't Jesus come in order to bring God's light to the world (starting with the Jews)? What better way to prove He was the One, the Messiah, than by floating down to the courtyard of the temple from a great height in front of all those people below? Yet Jesus—who loved even the hardest hearted Pharisee—wouldn't force them to see something with their eyes that their hearts didn't want to believe. (Could it be because it wouldn't have been *faith* if He dragged them to a conclusion?)

The devil also took Jesus up to a mountain and there showed him in an instant all the kingdoms of the world. And he said to him, "I will give you all their authority and splendor; it has been given to me, and I can give it to anyone I want to. If you worship me, it will all be yours." Jesus again refused.

All Jesus had to do to get them back was bow (and I'm told the language here implies Jesus would only have had to bow *once*). What a deal! No suffering, no rejection, no beating, no cross! Just bow once in worship. Satan was willing to transfer ownership of all the slaves (including you and me) who had been (and would be) born into slavery—in exchange for a bended knee. Satan's offer to Jesus would allow Him to skip the pain and get right to the object of His affection.

So . . . *was* the mighty Lord Jesus looking for slaves to drag along in His wake? Or was He looking for a bride . . . ransomed *from* slavery, delivered unto God without spot or wrinkle, filled with love for Her Bridegroom, as submitted to (and dependent upon) Him as He was to Father God? Would He settle for dragging a captive with no choice to the altar—OR would he be willing to empty out all that He had in sacrifice for a Bride who would love Him back? We have our answer in the cross. He makes the offer . . . "Come. All who are thirsty, weary, weak. Come to me." The choice is yours.

> **Galatians 5:1 Christ has set us free to live a free life. So take your stand! Never again let anyone put a harness of slavery on you.**—The Message

I don't know what the above says to you . . . but it says I've been set FREE from the bondage of slavery (not unwillingly dragged to another master). Thank You Jesus!!!!! With all my heart I praise You! What a Savior You are!

Other Demonstrations of Jesus' Intent

The Gospel of John (Chapter 6) records that, during His ministry there was a point when masses of people were following Jesus . . . until He said something that offended them. He said that He was manna from Heaven, and that the true manna was His flesh . . . and if they wouldn't partake of it, they weren't His.

John 6:50-52 But here is the bread that comes down from heaven, which **anyone *may*** eat and not die. 51 I am the living bread that came down from heaven. **Whoever** eats this bread will live forever. This bread is my flesh, which I will give for the life of the world."

52 Then the Jews began to argue sharply among themselves, "How can this man give us his flesh to eat?"

Then Jesus states the whole idea of Him being the bread once again . . . and then Scripture says,

From this time many of his disciples turned back and no longer followed him. [John 6:66]

Did He (who said right there that the bread of His flesh was given for "the life of the *world"*) chase them down and *drag* them back? Nope.

On the night before Jesus went to the cross, Peter (the one who said He was willing to die with Jesus!) denied even *knowing* Him. After the crucifixion, the Gospel of Mark (16:7) records that three women went to the tomb with spices to anoint the body of Jesus and were told by an angel,

> "You are looking for Jesus the Nazarene, who was crucified. He has risen! He is not here. See the place where they laid him. But go, tell his disciples *and Peter*, 'He is going ahead of you into Galilee. There you will see him, just as he told you.'"

I notice that Peter, who probably thought he'd fallen from all possibility of rescue, was specifically invited. Woo Hoo! But did Jesus go and *get* Peter and drag him to the meeting? No.

I can't think of a single place where Jesus dragged anyone *anywhere*. Neither did He cajole or manipulate them into following Him—nor did He limit their ability to walk away.

Which is more consistent with love: *Draw*, or *drag*? You decide.

With "draw" vs. "drag" in mind—wanting to represent Jesus' heart and words as accurately as possible—weigh the *context* of Jesus words in the surrounding text, within the Gospel of John, within His life and ministry. In John 12, Jesus talks about the cross as His manner of death. In John 3, Jesus says that it's because God so loved us that He was sent, and that it's by *faith* (choosing to believe that Jesus is our provision, or ransom for sin) we are saved. Then Jesus compares this provision (His manner of death, the cross) to the snake on the pole (Numbers 21:6-9) where people sinned against God and were bitten by poisonous snakes, but could look at the snake on the pole (believe God's provision) and live. He further says that "whoever does not believe stands condemned already because they have not believed in the name of God's one and only Son."

I want you, just for a moment, to put yourself in the place of a translator. I want you to think about the word "drag" vs. the word "draw" and look at the verse again and ask yourself, which seems the more appropriate word here?

"And I, when I am lifted up from the earth, will *drag* all people to myself."

As opposed to,

"And I, when I am lifted up from the earth, will *draw* all people to myself."

I think the translators got it right when they used the word "draw." I personally believe (and you can choose to disagree) that in THIS life, you choose whom you will serve. While you yet walk this earth, you are given opportunities each day to decide where you will abide in eternity.

Does the Bible speak of the salvation/reconciliation of all sentient beings (which could include demons and Satan)?

Rob Bell, in his book *Love Wins* states that "since the first church," and "at the center of the Christian tradition," there have been a number of people who thought everyone would be reconciled to God. [xliii] We will address Rob's version of "history" in Chapter Eleven but I wanted to show you that the idea "all will be reconciled" has momentum.

Carlton Pearson says that "God sees Himself, in everybody, in every belief system, in every icon, perhaps even the devil."[xliv] (Although Mr. Pearson has gone so far in his beliefs that I'm not even sure if other teachers of UR would want to stand shoulder to shoulder with him in a photo op.)

The Christian Universalist Association states that the cornerstone of their belief is the idea that there is no eternal hell, that "God has planned a positive outcome for all sentient beings." [xlv]

Before continuing, I have to note the statement: "God has planned the universe to produce a positive outcome for all sentient beings He has ever created." Where is this idea written? It may be a *hope* or a *conjecture* of people in the CUA, but it is not based on any clear statement in Scripture.

However, the CUA provides a list of scripture verses ("Jer. 31:38-40, Ezek. 16:53, Mat. 19:28, Acts 3:21") that are said to be "hopeful prophecies" (pointing to the positive outcome for all sentient beings). I understand that typos and other things happen, so in a list of references an unintentional mistake is no big deal—but <u>none</u> of the verses listed are references to Universalism. Whether the people at the Christian Universalist Association actually believe their list of verses prove their case or they merely believe no one will check the references is not clear, but let's actually look at them. Here are the actual verses corresponding to the list on their Universal Salvation page [xlvi] on the days that I accessed it:

> **Jer. 31:38-40** "The days are coming," declares the LORD, "when this city will be rebuilt for me from the Tower of Hananel to the Corner Gate. The measuring line will stretch from there straight to the hill of Gareb and then turn to Goah. The whole valley where dead bodies and ashes are thrown, and all the terraces out to the Kidron Valley on the east as far as the corner of the Horse Gate, will be holy to the LORD. The city will never again be uprooted or demolished."

As far as I can see, the above is about the future of the city of Jerusalem, not "universal restoration and renewal." The next Scripture on their list is *half* of a sentence:

> **Ezek. 16:53** "However, I will restore the fortunes of Sodom and her daughters and of Samaria and her daughters, and your fortunes along with them . . ."

---

xliii Rob Bell, *Love Wins, A Book About Heaven, Hell, and the Fate of Every Person Who Ever Lived*, (New York HarperCollins Publishers 2011) 109.

xliv http://www.beliefnet.com/Faiths/2003/06/Jesus-Will-Save-You-Whether-You-Agree-Or-Not.aspx#ixzz1zrqAzbQ 5 (June 5, 2012)

xlv From the *Universal Salvation* page of the Christian Universalist Assoc. website at http://www.christianuniversalist.org/articles/universalsalvation.html (16 Feb. 2012)

xlvi From the Universal Salvation page of the Christian Universalist Assoc. website at http://www.christianuniversalist.org/articles/universalsalvation.html (16 Feb. 2012)

Possibly "hopeful" . . . until you read the OTHER half of the sentence (not listed in the reference):

> **Ezekiel 16:54** "so that you may bear your disgrace and be ashamed of all you have done in giving them comfort."

Hardly a view of a happily-ever-after when you see the whole sentence. Here's the next verse they list:

> **Matt.19:28** So Jesus said to them, "Assuredly I say to you, that *in the regeneration*, when the Son of Man sits on the throne of His glory, you who have followed Me will also sit on twelve thrones, judging the twelve tribes of Israel."—KJV

The New International Version *does* say "renewal of all things" but it is the only version I found that does so. Other translations say "in the regeneration." Either way, the regeneration/renewal cannot be proven to apply to "the whole world."

The next verse they list is this one:

> **Acts 3:21** "Heaven must receive him until the time comes for God to restore everything, as he promised long ago through his holy prophets."

This verse *could* be seen as alluding to a Universalistic "restore everything"—until you read it in context. I cover their use of this verse on page 63 so I won't do it twice, but I want to say here, the subject of this verse isn't about everyone in the world going to heaven.

In addition, let me present the following Scripture about the purpose of listening to Jesus and accepting Him:

> **2 Corinthians 5:17-21** Therefore, if anyone is in Christ, the new creation has come: The old has gone, the new is here! 18 All this is from God, who reconciled us to himself through Christ and gave us the ministry of reconciliation: 19 that God was reconciling the world to himself in Christ, not counting people's sins against them. And he has committed to us the message of reconciliation. 20 We are therefore Christ's ambassadors, as though God were making his appeal through us. We implore you on Christ's behalf: *Be reconciled to God.* 21 God made him who had no sin to be sin for us, so that in him we *might* become the righteousness of God.
>
> *Please note the word "appeal." Is this consistent with the word "draw" or the word "drag"? Does the word "reconcile" speak of "drawing" people together or "dragging" them together?

Those who have accepted the gospel of Jesus Christ are now to go and give that same *appeal*— an appeal to repent (turn away from the ways, means, and promises of this world), to believe in the death and resurrection of Jesus on their behalf—and *ask* people to be reconciled to God. THAT is a message that is consistent throughout the entire Bible. As far as I can see, restoration, reconciliation, and renewal, aren't just—*poof*—imparted without the knowledge or consent of those involved, NOR are people "dragged" to Heaven. Salvation is available to all, but comes by faith, and faith comes through hearing the word of God.

Do any of the Scriptures the Christian Universalist Association lists truly depict what they claim? I don't think so. But on the same page as the above, the CUA goes on to say that at the end of all things there will be a "state of blessed reunion with God, the Creator . . . not eternal separation, misery or destruction" followed by another list of Bible verses (no text, just the listing of verses): John 12:32, Rom. 11:36, 1 Cor. 15:22,28, Col. 1:20, Rev. 21:3-5.[xlvii]

Let me write out the verses for you:

John 12:32 [Jesus speaking] "And I, when I am lifted up from the earth, will draw all people to myself."

(Note: We covered Universalism's version of the above verse earlier in this chapter. If you just skipped to this portion of the book you may want to check out pages 54 and 55 since they have a particular view of this verse.)

Moving on to the next verse in their list:

Rom. 11:36 For from him and through him and for him are all things. To him be the glory forever! Amen.

The above is a little abstract (with reference to their argument) but, okay. By itself, it could maybe mean what they think it means (everyone happily united with God). However, the whole discourse leading up to it is about salvation through faith and being cut off through unbelief, so I wouldn't say this passage supported their view. Let's go to their next verse:

1 Cor. 15:22, 28 For as in Adam all die, so in Christ all will be made alive. . . . (vs. 28) When he has done this, then the Son himself will be made subject to him who put everything under him, so that God may be all in all.

I will acknowledge that the above verses, disconnected from a Bible and floating here on the page are impressive! If you read these and nothing else in the New Testament, you can see their idea. But, here comes the need for context again.

IN CONTEXT, Paul was talking to the people of Corinth about two issues. First: Will there be a resurrection from the dead? Second: Has CHRIST been raised from the dead? He said that IF there was NO resurrection (as someone had claimed to the people of Corinth) then Christians were to be pitied above all people because they were still in their sins and those who had "fallen asleep in Christ" (a term applied to the righteous who had died) were "lost."

Let's see more of what Paul actually said in this passage:

1 Corinthians 15:20-25 But Christ has indeed been raised from the dead, the firstfruits of those who have <u>fallen asleep</u>. 21 For since death came through a man, the resurrection of the dead comes also through a man. 22 For as in Adam all die, so in Christ all will be made alive. 23 But each in turn: Christ, the firstfruits; *then, when he comes, those who belong to him*. 24 Then the end will come, when he hands over the kingdom to God the Father after he has destroyed all dominion, authority and power. 25 For he must reign until he has put all his enemies under his feet.

JUST TO CONSIDER the alternate view at this point, let's give the Universalist idea a little thought. What if, when Christ was raised from the dead, this shock wave of salvation just emanated out in all directions on earth and through time, saving everyone. *Boom!* You're saved (or will be). Add to this the Scriptures that say that ALL people will be resurrected. So you *could* read Universalism (not directly stated) INTO the above scripture.

[xlvii] From the Universal Salvation page of the Christian Universalist Assoc. website http://www.christianuniversalist.org/articles/universalsalvation.html (16 Feb. 2012

But let's look at another place where Jesus himself spoke about FAITH (or the lack thereof) and how it relates to the resurrection of *all* people:

> **John 5:19-30** Jesus gave them this answer: "Very truly I tell you, the Son can do nothing by himself; he can do only what he sees his Father doing, because whatever the Father does the Son also does. 20 For the Father loves the Son and shows him all he does. Yes, and he will show him even greater works than these, so that you will be amazed. 21 <u>For just as the Father raises the dead and gives them life, even so the Son gives life to whom he is pleased to give it.</u> 22 Moreover, <u>the Father judges no one, but has entrusted all judgment to the Son, 23 that all may honor the Son just as they honor the Father. Whoever does not honor the Son does not honor the Father, who sent him.</u>
>
> 24 "Very truly I tell you, *whoever hears my word and believes him who sent me* <u>has eternal life and will not be judged but has crossed over from death to life.</u> 25 Very truly I tell you, <u>a time is coming and has now come when the dead will hear the voice of the Son of God and those who hear will live.</u> 26 For as the Father has life in himself, so he has granted the Son also to have life in himself. 27 And he has given him authority to judge because he is the Son of Man.
>
> 28 "<u>Do not be amazed at this, for **a time is coming when *all* who are in their graves will hear his voice 29 and come out**—those who have done what is good will rise to live, and those who have done what is evil will rise to be condemned.</u> 30 By myself I can do nothing; I judge only as I hear, and my judgment is just, for I seek not to please myself but him who sent me."

Let's recap what Jesus said:

1) ALL people are to honor the Son as they honor the Father. Whoever does not honor the Son does not honor the Father (which implies choice).

2) Whoever <u>believes</u> Jesus' words and believes Father God has crossed over from death to life and will not be judged.

3) **ALL** will be resurrected, some to (new) life, and some to condemnation.

These aren't *my* boundaries, but those of Jesus Christ—and they are consistent with the theme of the entire New Testament.

In the books of Mark and John, we can read the sobering words Jesus said about Judas (the man who betrayed Him):

> "The Son of Man will go just as it is written about him. But woe to that man who betrays the Son of Man! It would be better for him if he had not been born." Mark 14:21 (also in Matthew 26:24)

YES, Jesus died for all—but each of us must <u>choose</u> to accept (believe and receive) the <u>offer</u> of salvation that is made <u>available</u> to us through the Gospel of Jesus Christ.

Titus 2:11 For the grace of God has appeared that *offers* salvation *to all people.*

Romans 2:7-8 He will give eternal life to those who keep on doing good, seeking after the glory and honor and immortality that God *offers.* 8 But he will pour out his anger and wrath on those who live for themselves, who refuse to obey the truth and instead live lives of wickedness.—NLT

Now, continuing on with the verses cited by the Christian Universalist Association (the verses they say support the idea that "the end of all things is a state of blessed reunion with God . . . not eternal separation, misery or destruction"):

Colossians 1:20 and through him to reconcile to himself all things, whether things on earth or things in heaven, by making peace through his blood, shed on the cross.

The above is another verse that *seems* to make their point! . . . But let's see it in context:

Colossians 1:19-23 For God was pleased to have all his fullness dwell in him, 20 and through him to reconcile to himself all things, whether things on earth or things in heaven, by making peace through his blood, shed on the cross. 21 Once you were alienated from God and were enemies in your minds because of your evil behavior. 22 But now he has reconciled you by Christ's physical body through death to present you holy in his sight, without blemish and free from accusation— 23 *if you continue in your faith*, established and firm, and do not move from the hope held out in the gospel.

Again, is Paul saying everyone is saved OR that salvation is *available* to everyone and is ours IF we continue in faith?

Lastly, they list another great passage from the end of the Bible, in the book of Revelation that *could* be seen as saying "in the end, it's all good" . . . *if it had no other verses around it.*

Revelation 21:3-5a And I heard a loud voice from the throne saying, "Look! God's dwelling place is now among the people, and he will dwell with them. They will be his people, and God himself will be with them and be their God. 4 'He will wipe every tear from their eyes. There will be no more death' or mourning or crying or pain, for the old order of things has passed away." 5 He who was seated on the throne said, "I am making everything new!"

But please read what *follows* those verses:

Revelation 21:5-8 He who was seated on the throne said, "I am making everything new!" Then he said, "Write this down, for these words are trustworthy and true." 6 He said to me: "It is done. I am the Alpha and the Omega, the Beginning and the End. To the thirsty I will give water without cost from the spring of the water of life. 7 Those who are victorious will inherit all this, and I will be their God and they will be my children. 8 But the cowardly, the unbelieving, the vile, the murderers, the sexually immoral, those who practice magic arts, the idolaters and all liars—they will be consigned to the fiery lake of burning sulfur. This is the *second* death."

In context, their snippet doesn't exactly say what they want it to say, does it?

Let's give one last look at the paragraph where the Christian Universalist Association listed these scriptures together as their reason to hope that all are saved:

> "The end of all things is a state of blessed reunion with God, the Creator -- not eternal separation, misery, or destruction. . . . In the early Christian church, this was called *apokatastasis* -- the reconciliation of all things -- and it was recognized as an important teaching of the Gospel during the first few centuries of Christianity."[xlviii]

I don't know a nice way to say it. If you read the verses they list *in context*, the Universalist picture (of God dragging all people to Heaven regardless of their will, regardless of their choices in this life) is not there.

As to the claim that their version of this reconciliation, "*apokatastasis,*" was recognized as an "important" teaching of the Gospel during the first few centuries of Christianity . . . we will further discuss the history of this thought later (in Chapter Eleven) but here are some of the problems I have with their definition/use of it being considered a Biblical one:

1. The Greek word *apokatastasis* appears ONCE in the New Testament (Acts 3:21)!
2. The word *apokatastasis,* is translated in *Strong's Exhaustive Concordance* as, "restitution."[xlix] In the *Thayer and Smith Greek Lexicon* it is translated as:
   restoration of a true theocracy,
   of the perfect state before the fall[l]
3. IN the CONTEXT of Acts 3, the **one-time use of the word** (which I have underlined below) *doesn't* say what Universalists want people to think it does. Let's read it:

   Acts 3:19-23 "19 Repent, then, and turn to God, so that your sins may be wiped out, that times of refreshing may come from the Lord, 20 and that he may send the Messiah, who has been appointed for you—even Jesus. 21 Heaven must receive him until the time comes for God to **restore** everything, as he promised long ago through his holy prophets. 22 For Moses said, 'The Lord your God will raise up for you a prophet like me from among your own people; you must listen to everything he tells you. 23 Anyone who does not listen to him* will be completely cut off from their people.'"

   * the "him" here refers to Jesus Christ.

The idea of the *necessity of repentance and heeding God's word* is given right there in connection to the "restoration." It says that the people must listen to everything the Messiah, Jesus, tells them. It also says those who don't listen will be completely cut off from their people. In context, the "restoration" of "everything" doesn't mean what Universalists think it does.

This is how an *assumption* about a *possible* definition of a single word which is only used once in the Bible becomes an entire doctrine.

---

xlviii From the Universal Salvation page of the Christian Universalist Assoc. website http://www.christianuniversalist.org/articles/universalsalvation.html (16 Feb. 2012)

xlix "*apokastasis*" #605, Strong's Exhaustive Concordance of the Bible, ©1800 by James Strong, Public Domain

l Thayer and Smith. Greek Lexicon entry for "*Apokatastasis*" The KJV New Testament Greek Lexicon, Public Domain (May 25, 2012)

CHAPTER 7—Lost in Translation?

One of the ways to cast doubt on a verse of Scripture is to say that the translation is faulty. To be sure, *no human language completely flows into another without some difficulties.* In English, we say "love" to denote our fondness for our spouse, our enjoyment of a book, and our craving for ice cream. In Greek, there are many words for love, each denoting a different variation or degree of it. Does that mean translation of any kind is impossible? No, but it needs to be done with a full grasp of both the language you are translating from and the one you are translating to. In addition, it's not solely about mechanical transcription of words, but about conveying the *heart* of what was meant in the original passage. Sometimes that requires a much broader perspective than just a single sentence or word.

Yes. I do believe that there are places in the Bible where teachers have misunderstood or redirected God's true intent over spans of history. (Some examples are the issue of slavery, the treatment of women, the meaning of "predestination," and the meaning of "prosperity"). But if you want REAL CLARITY about what God is saying, look at what He is also *doing*/has done. Jesus continually connects actions and the true intent of the heart. If there has been a mistranslation, misinterpretation, or misapplication, it can often be sorted out by looking at God's actions and the larger picture of the whole Bible. God is *not* the author of confusion or contradiction. If you have verses of Scripture that appear to be at war with each other . . . look at the context and what God does. If the Bible repeatedly says that those who don't abide (remain, walk, tarry, endure) in Him will suffer fire/destruction/condemnation . . . I don't think we should take it lightly or dismiss it.

Is it *FOREVER* or TEMPORARY?

In the Universalist and Universal Reconciliation movements, much ado has been made over the words translated "forever," "everlasting," and "eternal" in the New Testament. The contention of Universalists and those in UR is that the words "aion and "aionios" (the words translated "forever," "everlasting," and "eternal" in English) can sometimes be used to mean limited amounts of time (such as an "age"), therefore, regarding devastation or punishment, Universalists have chosen to believe those words denote a limited period of time. They declare that, regarding Hell, Christians have been misled "based on mistranslations of the Bible."[li]

Most of the Universalist/UR literature I've seen states that when it comes to punishment or justice or hell, God only means those to last "an age." One of the reasons for this is reflected in this quote from the Christian Universalist Association:

> "Proportionality also ensures that any judgments upon a soul by God must be temporary and limited, since the sin that caused those judgments to ensue was also limited. This is a basic, Biblical teaching about divine justice -- and it is also common sense."[lii]

[li] http://www.christianuniversalist.org/articles/justice-afterlife.html (June 5, 2012) —but similar thoughts are also found at other Universalist sites such as http://www.tentmaker.org/books/infinitegrace.htm, http://www.urqa.com/index.html, http://www.hopebeyondhell.net/hope-beyond-hell-11-eternity-b/

[lii] From the Christian Universalist Association website http://www.christianuniversalist.org/articles/justice-afterlife.html (13 October 2011)

"Proportionality." Well. That's a fine word, isn't it? What does it mean? It means one thing having the correct relationship of size, quantity, or degree to something else. According to CUA, proportionality "ensures" (guarantees) that divine justice and punishment are "limited." So . . . are they saying that if you were just a wee bit sinful, your punishment should be small as well?

Before I give my own thoughts here, I want to quote what I thought was an *excellent* article by Matthew Raley, entitled *God's Redemptive Justice*:

> Is it the case that redemptive mercy is central to God's character, and does this characteristic invalidate the idea of hell?
>
> Let's probe the word redemption. The Greek word is *lutron*, which refers to the ransom price for slaves or captives. There will be no release until the price is paid. Jesus, speaking about the key to his Lordship, says that he came to serve by giving his life as the redemption price for many (Mark 10.35-45).
>
> Another word that expresses a similar idea is propitiation. Paul teaches that God made Christ's blood to be the "propitiation," the appeasement of God's justice, that sinners receive by faith (Romans 3.21-26). . . . That is, God's justice is demonstrated by his paying the price incurred by sin.
>
> God does not do "remedial" sentences as a way to satisfy his justice. When he shows mercy to a sinner, he purchases the individual out of death into life. . . .
>
> In other words, Christ's death on the cross was redemptive because the death was entirely punitive. In God's plan the cross was not a sympathy-generating symbol or an attention-getting drama. It was the final propitiation of God's wrath. It paid the ransom.
>
> I have never been impressed with modernism's treasured fantasy of cultural progress. Today's notion of remedial justice is founded on the lie that sin is not truly destructive of human life. Believing lies like this is not a sign of evolutionary refinement, but of degradation. <u>Sin is destructive, and its deadly consequences cry out for recompense. The fact that we are all under sentence only makes the urgency of the cross more intense.</u>[liii] [Underline added by me]

How a "limited time" (a.k.a. "proportional" Hell) argument further loses merit

There are at least four arenas where the "limited time" argument falls down (and we will consider each area):
1. Placing things in context,
2. "Degrees" of sin equals degrees of punishment,
3. Limits of understanding, and
4. Limits of language.

[liii] Matthew Raley, *God's Redemptive Justice*, on the site Tritone Life, http://tritonelife.com/2011/04/26/gods-redemptive-justice/ posted April 26, 2011, accessed March 29, 2012 quote used with permission

1. CONTEXT—Why "Forever" isn't Temporary

As some claim, does the Greek word "*aionios*" only mean "a distinct age or period of time with a beginning and an end?" The answer to that is NO.

But, *is there some wiggle room* when it comes to the words translated "forever," "everlasting," and "eternal"?

Yes. In that the word has multiple possible usages (of varying duration) there *could* be some wiggle room, especially if one only uses select verses where the case for "a limited age" could be made. HOWEVER, one of the reasons translators chose the words "forever," "eternal," and "everlasting" when translating these passages was because **Jesus Himself** placed them in conjunction with other terms that gave finality, completeness, and/or permanence to the idea of punishment. Below are statements made by Jesus that contradict the "temporary" concept promoted by Universalists and people in UR. Please note that there are more passages in the Old and New Testaments that line up with these—but I have used quotes from Jesus, in hopes of keeping to the heart of the matter.

Before your read the following, ask yourself:

1. *Did Jesus ever say something that was idle chatter?*
2. *Does Jesus need to engage in empty threats or manipulation to accomplish a goal?*
3. *Did Jesus ever tell a parable or story in public and then, in private, say it meant something totally opposite?*

If the answer to these questions is, "No," then we must hear His words—not only on the great mercy, healing, and love He purchased for us but also the words on *what* He judges, *when* He judges, and *whom* He judges.

> **Matthew 5:20** [Jesus speaking] "For I tell you that unless your righteousness surpasses that of the Pharisees and the teachers of the law, you will certainly not* enter the kingdom of heaven."
>
> **Matthew 18:33** And he [Jesus] said: "Truly I tell you, unless you change and become like little children, you will never* enter the kingdom of heaven."
>
> **Mark 10:15** [Jesus speaking] "Truly I tell you, anyone who will not receive the kingdom of God like a little child will never* enter it."
>
> **Luke 18:17** [Jesus speaking] "I tell you the truth, anyone who doesn't receive the Kingdom of God like a child will never* enter it."
>
> *Strong's #3364—never, certainly not, not at all, by no means "A double negative strengthening the denial—not at all."[liv]

Here are more words of Jesus that give us the sense of absoluteness when it comes to judgment.

> **Matthew 10:32-33** [Jesus speaking] "Everyone who acknowledges me publicly here on earth, I will also acknowledge before my Father in heaven. 33 But everyone who denies me here on earth, I will also deny before my Father in heaven."

[liv] Ref. #3364, James Strong, *Strong's Exhaustive Concordance of the Bible*, 1800, Public Domain

Matthew 12:30-32 [Jesus speaking] "Whoever is not with me is against me, and whoever does not gather with me scatters. 31 And so I tell you, every kind of sin and slander can be forgiven, but blasphemy against the Spirit will not be forgiven. 32 Anyone who speaks a word against the Son of Man will be forgiven, <u>but anyone who speaks against the Holy Spirit will not be forgiven</u>, **either in this age *or* in the age to come**."

Luke 12:10 [Jesus speaking] "And everyone who speaks a word against the Son of Man will be forgiven, <u>but anyone who blasphemes against the Holy Spirit</u> **will not be forgiven**."

John 3:35-36 [Jesus speaking] "The Father loves the Son and has placed everything in his hands. 36 Whoever believes in the Son has eternal life, <u>but whoever rejects the Son will not see life, for God's wrath remains* on them.</u>"

> *"remains"—Strong's # 3306 *menw* a primary verb; to stay (in a given place, state, relation or expectancy):—abide, continue, dwell, endure, be present, remain, stand, tarry[lv]

Mark 3:28-29 [Jesus speaking] "Truly I tell you, people can be forgiven all their sins and every slander they utter, but whoever blasphemes against the Holy Spirit will never be forgiven; they are guilty of an eternal sin."

Mark 9:42-48 [Jesus speaking] "If anyone causes one of these little ones—those who believe in me—to stumble, it would be better for them if a large millstone were hung around their neck and they were thrown into the sea. 43 If your hand causes you to stumble, cut it off. It is better for you to enter life maimed than with two hands to go into hell [Gehenna], where the <u>fire</u> never goes out. ** 45 And if your foot causes you to stumble, cut it off. It is better for you to enter life crippled than to have two feet and be thrown into hell [Gehenna]. And if your eye causes you to stumble, pluck it out. It is better for you to enter the kingdom of God with one eye than to have two eyes and be thrown into hell [Gehenna], where 'the worms that eat them do not die, and the <u>fire* is not quenched.</u>**'" (Word "Gehenna" in brackets [ ] added by me to show the word used.)

> ** The words "never goes out" and "not quenched" (Strong's ref. #762) *Asbestos* —
> 1. unquenched, unquenchable a. of eternal hell fire to punish the damned [lvi]

> In vs. 48 Jesus is a quoting from:
>> **Isaiah 66:24** "And they will go out and look on the dead bodies of those who rebelled against me; the worms that eat them will not die, the fire that burns them *will not be quenched*, and they will be loathsome to all mankind."

I realize that some will dispute whether or not Jesus was talking about the final judgment here, but—taken with all of His other statements, I believe it warrants *serious* thought.

Something Jesus took very seriously (and we should, too) because He tied it to *not* entering the kingdom of Heaven: *Denial*

Luke 12:9 [Jesus speaking] "But anyone who denies me here on earth will be denied before God's angels."—NLT

[lv] # 3306, James Strong, Strong's Exhaustive Concordance of the Bible, 1800, Public Domain

[lvi] #762, James Strong, Strong's Exhaustive Concordance of the Bible, 1800, Public Domain

Let's break that down. In the first half of the sentence, Jesus said, "But anyone who denies me here on earth . . ."

The word translated "denies" in the first part of the sentence is –

Strong's # 720 *arneomai*
   1) to deny
   2) to deny someone
      a) to deny one's self
         1. to disregard his own interests or to prove false to himself
         2. act entirely unlike himself
   3) to deny, abnegate, abjure
   4) not to accept, to reject, to refuse something <u>offered</u> [lvii]

In the second half of the sentence, (Jesus said, " . . . will be denied before God's angels.") The word translated "denied" here is different than the word translated "denies" in the first part of the sentence.

   Strong's #533 *aparneomai*

1) to deny
   a) to affirm that one has no acquaintance or connection with someone
   b) to forget one's self, lose sight of one's self and one's own interests [lviii]

So Jesus said, "He who denies me(disregards, rejects what is offered, refuses me) in front of men (the implication here is IN THIS LIFE) shall be denied (it will be affirmed that this person has no acquaintance or connection with Me) before the angels (in the age to come)." Those who deny Jesus in word or deed are not "known" by Him, they are not His friends or His disciples. Is this a one-time statement that might be misunderstood? Is it something that I am taking out of context? No.

Matthew 10:38 Whoever does not take up their cross and follow me is not worthy of me.

Matthew 16:24 Then Jesus said to his disciples, "Whoever wants to be my disciple must deny themselves and take up their cross and follow me."

Mark 8:34 Then he called the crowd to him along with his disciples and said: "Whoever wants to be my disciple must deny themselves and take up their cross and follow me."

Luke 9:23-26 And He was saying to them all, "If anyone wishes to come after Me, he must deny himself, and take up his cross daily and follow Me. 24 For whoever wishes to save his life will lose it, but whoever loses his life for My sake, he is the one who will save it. 25 For what is a man profited if he gains the whole world, and loses or forfeits himself? 26 For whoever is ashamed of Me and My words, the Son of Man will be ashamed of him when He comes in His glory, and the glory of the Father and of the holy angels."—NASB

Luke 14:27 "And whoever does not carry their cross and follow me cannot be my disciple."

James 1:12 Blessed is the one who perseveres under trial because, having stood the test, that person will receive the crown of life that the Lord has promised to those who love him.

---

lvii "deny" #720, James Strong, *Strong's Exhaustive Concordance of the Bible*, 1800, Public Domain

lviii "deny" #533, James Strong, *Strong's Exhaustive Concordance of the Bible*, 1800, Public Domain

Hebrews 10:39 But we do not belong to those who shrink back and are destroyed, but to those who have faith and are saved.

2 Timothy 2:10-13 Therefore I endure everything for the sake of the elect, that they too may obtain the salvation that is in Christ Jesus, with eternal glory. Here is a trustworthy saying: If we died with him, we will also live with him; if we endure, we will also reign with him. If we disown him, he will also disown us; if we are faithless, he remains faithful, for he cannot disown himself.

Titus 1:16 They claim to know God, but by their actions they deny him. They are detestable, disobedient and unfit for doing anything good.

Here are more statements made by Jesus that give no hint of a "temporary" shut out of the unrighteous.

Matthew 7:13-14 [Jesus speaking] "Enter through the narrow gate. For wide is the gate and broad is the road that leads to destruction, and many enter through it. But small is the gate and narrow the road that leads to life, and only a few find it."

Matthew 7:21-23 [Jesus speaking] "**Not everyone** who says to me, 'Lord, Lord,' will enter the kingdom of heaven, but only the one who does the will of my Father who is in heaven. 22 Many will say to me on that day, 'Lord, Lord, did we not prophesy in your name and in your name drive out demons and in your name perform many miracles?' 23 Then I will tell them plainly, 'I never knew you. Away from me, you evildoers!'" (Text bolded by me)

Luke 13:22-28 Then Jesus went through the towns and villages, teaching as he made his way to Jerusalem. 23 Someone asked him, "Lord, are only a few people going to be saved?"

He said to them, 24 "Make every effort to enter through the narrow door, because many, I tell you, will try to enter and will not be able to. 25 Once the owner of the house gets up and closes the door, you will stand outside knocking and pleading, 'Sir, open the door for us.' But he will answer, 'I don't know you or where you come from.' 26 "Then you will say, 'We ate and drank with you, and you taught in our streets.' 27 "But he will reply, 'I don't know you or where you come from. Away from me, all you evildoers!' 28 "There will be weeping there, and gnashing of teeth, when you see Abraham, Isaac and Jacob and all the prophets in the kingdom of God, but you yourselves thrown out. "

So we aren't talking about a few sundry verses where we could scratch out the word "eternal" or "everlasting" and replace it with "an age" or "a limited time" and all the other verses of the New Testament would just line up and still make sense. You would have to delete or change a substantial amount of Scripture *in addition to* the ones containing the words "eternal" and "everlasting" to make the Universalist/UR theory work.

2. "PROPORTIONALITY": The idea that "Degrees" of sin equals degrees of punishment

The Christian Universalist Association says, "Proportionality also ensures that any judgments upon a soul by God must be temporary and limited . . ."[lix]

[lix] From the Christian Universalist Association website http://www.christianuniversalist.org/articles/justice-afterlife.html (13 October 2011)

A vital concept has gone right over the head of anyone who believes that statement. God's sentence (the punishment) for sin/unbelief has always been one thing: Death. It isn't some limited, "proportional" thing. It's death. Unlike the movie *The Princess Bride* where someone could be "mostly dead" as compared to "all dead"—death is death. While we are still walking this earth, the consequences for sin (while painful) are limited—hopefully causing the sinful to repent before they die and face judgement[lx]. The only sure way to avoid God's sentence on sin (in the judgment yet to come) is to plead guilty, to find release under the blood of Jesus right now—and that is why Jesus commands us to share His gospel and make disciples in this life.

Universalists can come up with the concept of "proportionality" in some fashion in Scripture, but not in reference to the afterlife. Jesus Christ said MORE about judgment and Hell than about the rewards or the kingdom of Heaven, yet nowhere do I see Jesus teaching about proportional judgment of people who were just "a little bad" versus those who were "very bad." While *believers* may have to give an account for what they did with their time, efforts, and resources here, this won't be an issue that decides if they're going to Heaven or the lake of fire. What determines our eternity is where we put our faith! People are either saved by virtue of *faith* or they are not.

YOU AREN'T SAVED BY MERE HEAD KNOWLEDGE. *KNOWING* GOD, heart and soul, is EVERYTHING.

When The Bible speaks of people "knowing" God this is more than mere acknowledgement of His existence or memorization of facts about Him, it refers to an intimate fellowship, a communion that produces fruit. Adam *knew* Eve and they had children. If I know Jesus, I will walk with Him and my life will increasingly bear fruit that shows it. You either *know* God (and are known *by* Him) or you don't know Him and are not known by Him. Look up the number of places in the Gospels where (in the context of judgment) Jesus says, "*I don't know you.*"

3. The theory of limited CONCEPT: The idea that the limited understanding of ancient people limits what God meant/intended

To say that ancient people had no concept of eternity (and therefore couldn't have referenced it in the Bible) is misleading. Many scholars are convinced that Aristotle elaborated on the concept of eternity/infinity centuries before the incarnation of Christ. The Romans used the Greek terms, and there is evidence that the Jews had the concept of eternity as well. AND IF ANYBODY ever had an understanding of eternity . . . it was Jesus Christ.

4. Is REALITY somehow limited by LANGUAGE?

One argument of some Universalists is to say because people in antiquity didn't understand the concept of "eternal" and/or they had no exclusive, set aside word for *eternity* or the *infinite*, then "eternal" can't be accurately applied to punishment or Hell.

There are whole libraries of scientific books available on the topics of gravity and magnetism—yet *NO ONE on this planet today* fully understands how either of them works. Does the fact that we don't understand gravity or magnetism exempt us from their pull? No!

[lx] Hebrews 9:27

If the determining factor of something's actual existence is a writer's ability to fully comprehend it and coin an exclusive term for it, then *God* couldn't be a real topic of Scripture because no one fully understands Him, nor is there a complete single word in human language that defines Him.

Fact: Having an exclusive word for something doesn't determine whether or not it is accurately applied.

How many of the prophets in the Bible wrote of things they couldn't fully comprehend? How many saw events that wouldn't happen for centuries or even thousands of years, yet had the faith to believe and report what they had seen? I realize that there are those who love to rationalize away prophecy and the supernatural, but the fact is, they can't. Prophecy, miracles, the power of the shed blood of Jesus Christ, and the Lord Himself are all outside our abilities to fully grasp, yet we are asked by the Lord to believe. **That's what faith is.**

Perhaps without intending to do so, Universalists opened a can of worms with their argument that "*aionios*" only means eternal when it is applied to God, but the same word, applied to punishment, means a limited amount of time. They claim that God is an exception . . . because they've decided He is.

WHAT IF we looked at the words translated "all" and "world" for a moment.

I'd like to address a word that Universalists and those in UR use to assert their claim that all people are saved. The word "all" IS used several times (I believe it's only four or five times) in reference to salvation in addition to the word "world" which also appears many times in connection with the cross.

"ALL" and, in many instances, the word "WORLD"—are *both* the Greek word *pas* (*Strong's* #3956) and here are the definitions for it:
1. Individually—each, every, any, all, the whole, everyone, all things, everything
2. collectively –*some of all types* lxi

Please note the second definition, "some of all types." Examples of this would be:

> **Matthew 3:5-6** "They went out to him Jerusalem, and all Judaea, and all the region round about Jordan, And were baptized of him in Jordan, confessing their sins." [KJV]

Were *all* of the people of Judaea and of *all* the region round about Jordan baptized by John as the King James Version says? No. The misconception was straightened out in later translations, but do you see how it can be made to say something *other* than intended?

Here is example of the use of "the whole world" in the New International Version:

> **John 12:19** So the Pharisees said to one another, "See, this is getting us nowhere. Look how the whole world has gone after him!"

Had the "whole world" gone after Jesus? No. But, in this case, it was a *dramatic expression* on the part of the Pharisees. They wouldn't really have cared what the *Gentiles* (the people outside of Judaism) were doing in the way of religion. What they cared about was that many Jews were following Jesus and it was a threat to their power.

---

lxi James Strong, *Strong's Exhaustive Concordance of the Bible*, 1800, Public Domain

Acts 2:46-47 Every day they continued to meet together in the temple courts. They broke bread in their homes and ate together with glad and sincere hearts, 47 praising God and *enjoying the favor of all the people*. And the Lord added to their number daily those who were being saved.

Did the first Christians in Jerusalem know the favor of "all" the people (as in everyone in Jerusalem or everyone for all time?) No. But there was a short season in which they knew the favor of the city in general.

There are probably more than a dozen such places that the words "all" or "world" could be easily located in the New Testament when something generally smaller than "all" or "world" is meant. Does that mean the words "all" and "world" in the Bible *never* actually mean ALL or the whole WORLD? No—in fact they most often DO convey the largest meaning.

Despite the fact that the word "all" could generally be used to depict something less than "totally" doesn't limit the use of it. The keys to REAL proof are context and consistency (of word and deed).

So when a person in Universal Reconciliation quotes something like Romans 5:18 ("just as one trespass resulted in condemnation for **all** people, so also one righteous act resulted in justification and life for **all** people") and says that this is proof that all of humanity is saved, I'm not wooed by it. Both Old and New Testaments say that ALL of us need saving. And, IN CONTEXT, the *vast* amount of New Testament Scripture on the topic of salvation says that, while it has been purchased *for all* by Jesus . . . *not all* will accept it.

Here is that verse in the Amplified Version which gives further understanding for words and terms in parentheses and brackets.

Romans 5:18 Well then, as one man's trespass [one man's false step and falling away led] to condemnation for all men, so one Man's act of righteousness [leads] to acquittal and right standing with God and life for all men.—Amplified Bible

By the way, did you see the word "leads" in brackets there? It tells us what the implication of the original Greek is. Let's think about that a moment: *Leads*. Is that consistent with the word "draw" or with the word "drag"? :-)

What IS a METAPHOR anyway?

Universalists' Perspective on the "warning" of Sodom and Gomorrah

I've read Universalist (UR) writings that see it like this: Sodom and Gomorrah were "destroyed" but they aren't still burning (eternally) so if Hell is compared to Sodom . . . it's not eternal.[lxii] I've also read UR writings that statements Jesus made about people being thrown into Gehenna correlate to an actual valley outside Jerusalem where all the refuse was burned—and say that since Gehenna was an actual, physical place where the fire, worms, etc. were limited, then Hell is similarly limited.

Is there wiggle room?

[lxii] An example of this teaching is a free book, *The Outcome of Infinite Grace*, by Dr. Loyal Hurley at www.tentmaker.org/books/infinite grace.htm

According to the Mirriam-Webster's Dictionary, a metaphor is:

1.: a figure of speech in which a word or phrase literally denoting one kind of object or idea is used in place of another **to suggest a likeness or analogy** between them (as in drowning in money); broadly : figurative language — compare simile [lxiii] [bold added by me for emphasis]

As with ANY form of communication, the use of metaphors (or parables, or types, or shadows) is complicated by the following:

1. The continuing evolution in the meaning of specific words. As we saw in the little quotation about Constance at the beginning of CHAPTER 4, what a word means in one time or culture isn't necessarily what it will mean even ten years later!
2. The evolution of culture, society, customs, and technology. Jesus taught using examples of life that were typical to the time and place. People were familiar with bridal customs, things that were considered taboo, land rights, the laws of inheritance, etc.

Most people today are disconnected from the rural life that was common in Bible times. We don't readily understand the metaphors and parables about sheep, shepherds, vineyards, planting seeds, and harvests. A little research can give a wealth of understanding . . . but many are content to just skip over those passages or to let someone else interpret the meaning.

There will ALWAYS be difficulty in relating something that *cannot* be completely grasped to something that *can*. The fact remains, however, that metaphors are a proven, valuable tool of communication and God used them all the time. To get our message across, we all will point to something understood or seen and say "it's sort of *like* this." Jesus used the canvas of life and nature to paint pictures—and then said, "This is what the Kingdom of God is *like*," or "this is what faith is *like*."

When speaking to Nicodemus, Jesus compared the Holy Spirit to wind, which at the time couldn't be tracked or predicted with any degree of certainty. Today, technology lets us "see" where the wind came from, and predict where it's going (often with quite a bit of accuracy). Does that mean the Holy Spirit is now limited? No! Jesus was simply using a concept to illustrate the power of God so that Nicodemus would have something to wrap his brain around.

We must realize that there is an ever-present temptation to make the metaphor mean something more, less, or *other* than what God intended. One of the best means of holding the message of the metaphor intact is the context—where the words were said, to whom, about what or whom . . . and what are the actions of God that give further context?

> Beloved, Christianity is NOT a secret society where people must search for secrets or hidden meanings in order to find eternal life. Cults are formed when someone claims to have a tidbit of information that isn't supplied in the Bible but essentially changes the meaning of what is there.

Sodom and Gomorrah—the New Testament repeatedly states that what happened in these cities should serve as a *warning* to rebellious and hard-hearted people. The fact that Jesus said so much about punishment says to me that He was taking it seriously, that He wanted people to know there

---

lxiii "metaphor." Merriam-Webster.com. 2011. http://www.merriam-webster.com (16 February 2012).

will be consequences for what they choose here. It's not our job to discount or minimize what He said.

Both the Bible <u>and</u> perspectives of Church doctrine in the first century point to something much more serious than the happy outcome Universalists predict. While I think it's wrong to "preach Hell" (make avoiding Hell the focus of salvation), I also believe it's wrong to dismiss the witness of Jesus Christ, of the early Church, and the New Testament as all being mistaken.

Having said (and quoted) all this, I will say that *God is GOD*.

Nothing is impossible for God. But IF there is some plan to eventually let everyone into Heaven, <u>it's not something we've been asked to believe *or* told to promote.</u> There is <u>no solid offer or means</u> for it set forth in the Bible—and to give people the impression that there IS one is to deny the clear statements that Jesus made, telling us to call people to HIS kingdom, to make disciples who would walk with Him.

CHAPTER 8—What IS the "faith" that saves people?

One of the definitions of "faith" in Oxford's online dictionary is "strong belief . . . based on spiritual conviction rather than proof."[lxiv]

So, even according to the dictionary, "faith" is trust or belief (in God or something else) for what we cannot see, or something we don't yet fully possess. The Bible says the same thing.

The unifying truth of the Old Testament and New Testament is that salvation comes through *faith*. From the opening pages of Genesis to the end of the Old Testament, we see that when people had "faith" in (believed) the promise of God, it was "reckoned to them as righteousness."

Genesis 15:6 Abram believed the LORD, and He credited it to him as righteousness.

In addition to Abraham, a famous passage of Hebrews, a long list of Old Testament saints is given:

Hebrews 11:13 All these people died still believing what God had promised them. They did not receive what was promised, but they saw it all from a distance and welcomed it. They agreed that they were foreigners and nomads here on earth. 14 Obviously people who say such things are looking forward to a country they can call their own. 15 If they had longed for the country they came from, they could have gone back. 16 But they were looking for a better place, a heavenly homeland. That is why God is not ashamed to be called their God, for he has prepared a city for them.

And now, we have Jesus Christ—who IS the Promise of God.

1 Timothy 1:15-17 It is a trustworthy statement, deserving full acceptance, that Christ Jesus came into the world to save sinners, among whom I am foremost of all. 16 Yet for this reason I found mercy, so that in me as the foremost, Jesus Christ might demonstrate His perfect patience as an example for those who would believe in Him for eternal life. 17 Now to the King eternal, immortal, invisible, the only God, be honor and glory forever and ever. Amen.—NASB

Romans 10:1-4 Brothers and sisters, my heart's desire and prayer to God for the Israelites is that they may be saved. 2 For I can testify about them that they are zealous for God, but their zeal is not based on knowledge. 3 Since they did not know the righteousness of God and sought to establish their own, they did not submit to God's righteousness. 4 **Christ is the culmination of the law so that there may be righteousness for everyone who believes**.

Romans 10:11-13 Scripture says, "Anyone who believes in him will never be put to shame."(*) 12 For there is no difference between Jew and Gentile—the same Lord is Lord of all and richly blesses all who call on him, 13 for, "Everyone who calls on the name of the Lord will be saved."(**)

(*) Also found in Isaiah 28:16
(**) Also found in Joel 2:32

---

lxiv "faith," *Oxfords Dictionary* online, http://oxforddictionaries.com/definition/faith?q=faith (February 21, 2012)

Romans 10:14-17 And that message is the very message about faith that we preach: 9 If you confess with your mouth that Jesus is Lord and believe in your heart that God raised him from the dead, you will be saved. 10 For it is by believing in your heart that you are made right with God, and it is by confessing with your mouth that you are saved. 11 As the Scriptures tell us, "Anyone who trusts in him will never be disgraced."

14 But how can they call on him to save them unless they believe in him? And how can they believe in him if they have never heard about him? And how can they hear about him unless someone tells them? 15 And how will anyone go and tell them without being sent? That is why the Scriptures say, "How beautiful are the feet of messengers who bring good news!"

16 But not everyone welcomes the Good News, for Isaiah the prophet said, "LORD, who has believed our message?" 17 <u>So faith comes from hearing, that is, hearing the Good News about Christ.</u>—NLT

Galatians 3:11 "So it is clear that no one can be made right with God by trying to keep the law. For the Scriptures say, "It is through faith that a righteous person has life."—NLT

Hebrews 10:35-39 So do not throw away this confident trust in the Lord. Remember the great reward it brings you! Patient endurance is what you need now, so that you will continue to do God's will. Then you will receive all that he has promised. "For in just a little while, the Coming One will come and not delay. And my righteous ones will live by faith. But I will take no pleasure in anyone who turns away." But we are not like those who turn away from God to their own destruction. We are the faithful ones, whose souls will be saved. —NLT

Faith in what or whom?

John 1:12-13 [speaking about Jesus] <u>Yet to all who did receive him, to those who believed in his name, he gave the right to become children of God—</u> 13 children born not of natural descent, nor of human decision or a husband's will, but born of God.

Matthew 12:46-50 While Jesus was still talking to the crowd, his mother and brothers stood outside, wanting to speak to him. 47 Someone told him, "Your mother and brothers are standing outside, wanting to speak to you." 48 He replied to him, "Who is my mother, and who are my brothers?" 49 Pointing to his disciples, he said, "Here are my mother and my brothers. 50 <u>For whoever does the will of my Father in heaven is my brother and sister and mother.</u>"

Ephesians 4:4-6 There is one body and one Spirit, just as you were called to one hope when you were called; 5 one Lord, one faith, one baptism; 6 one God and Father of all, who is over all and through all and in all.

Can Demons Have "Faith" That Saves?

In the Bible, salvation is inseparably linked with the (physical) life that people have here on this earth. Throughout the Bible, God equates our claims of faith and love to what we do *here*.[lxv] If fallen angels/demons will have a chance to repent, it's not something we are given to know. The purpose of the cross was to save humans. Angels are a separate creation from humans and their natural state is not in flesh like ours. Also, they have seen God, been in His presence—and faith is believing what one cannot see.

[lxv] An example would be Matthew 25:31-46—We don't *earn* Heaven, but our lives will *reflect* what we truly believe.

Hebrews 2:16-17 *We also know that the Son did not come to help angels;* he came to help the descendants of Abraham. 17 Therefore, it was necessary for him to be made in every respect like us, his brothers and sisters, so that he could be our merciful and faithful High Priest before God. Then he could offer a sacrifice that would take away the sins of the people.—NLT

The Gospel

The "gospel" as defined within the New Testament itself is the "good news" that Jesus died for our sins and rose again, and that we have life by believing in Him. When you read any New Testament verse containing the words "gospel" or "Good News" this is what the writer intended.

2 Timothy 2:8-9 Remember Jesus Christ, raised from the dead, descended from David. This is my gospel, for which I am suffering even to the point of being chained like a criminal.

Romans 1:16-17 For I am not ashamed of the gospel, because it is the power of God that brings salvation to everyone who believes: first to the Jew, then to the Gentile. For in the gospel the righteousness of God is revealed—a righteousness that is by faith from first to last, just as it is written: "The righteous will live by faith."* —NLT

*this is a reference to the O.T. Scripture: Habakkuk 2:4

Can/Does the Gospel "evolve"?

Certainly, I think we can come to a better understanding of what is said in the New Testament as we allow God's light to shine in our hearts, but I don't think the Gospel changes. While people may be more sophisticated and intellectual, our willingness to play with terms and our egos can be great impediments to faith.

I don't think there is any evidence to prove that God has changed the Way of salvation. I believe it was and is His desire for people be saved but there aren't multiple "plans" to do this. Scripture says there is only one faith, Body, baptism, God, Father, Shepherd, flock (Ephesians 4:4-6).

Galatians 6:6-9 I am shocked that you are turning away so soon from God, who called you to himself through the loving mercy of Christ. You are following a different way that pretends to be the Good News 7 but is not the Good News at all. You are being fooled by those who deliberately twist the truth concerning Christ. 8 Let God's curse fall on anyone, including us or even an angel from heaven, who preaches a different kind of Good News than the one we preached to you. 9 I say again what we have said before: If anyone preaches any other Good News than the one you welcomed, let that person be cursed.—NLT

Matthew 24:14 [Jesus speaking] "And this gospel of the kingdom will be preached in the whole world as a testimony to all nations, and then the end will come."

John 5:36-40 & 46 [Jesus speaking] "I have testimony weightier than that of John. For the works that the Father has given me to finish—the very works that I am doing—testify that the Father has sent me. 37 And the Father who sent me has himself testified concerning me. You have never heard his voice nor seen his form, 38 nor does his word dwell in you, for you do not believe the one he sent. 39 You study the Scriptures diligently because you think that in them you have eternal life. These are the very Scriptures that testify about me, 40 yet you refuse to come to me to have life. . . . 46 If you believed Moses, you would believe me, for he wrote about me."

Romans 10:11-13 Scripture says, "Anyone who believes in him will never be put to shame."(*) 12 For there is no difference between Jew and Gentile—the same Lord is Lord of all and richly blesses all who call on him, 13 for, "Everyone who calls on the name of the Lord will be saved."(**)

(*) Also found in Isaiah 28:16

(**) Also found in Joel 2:32

1 Corinthians 2:1-2 And so it was with me, brothers and sisters. When I came to you, I did not come with eloquence or human wisdom as I proclaimed to you the testimony about God. 2 For I resolved to know nothing while I was with you except Jesus Christ and him crucified.

1 Corinthians 3:10-15 By the grace God has given me, I laid a foundation as a wise builder, and someone else is building on it. But each one should build with care. 11 For no one can lay any foundation other than the one already laid, which is Jesus Christ. 12 If anyone builds on this foundation using gold, silver, costly stones, wood, hay or straw, 13 their work will be shown for what it is, because the Day will bring it to light. It will be revealed with fire, and the fire will test the quality of each person's work. 14 If what has been built survives, the builder will receive a reward. 15 If it is burned up, the builder will suffer loss but yet will be saved—even though only as one escaping through the flames.

2 Timothy 1:8 So do not be ashamed of the testimony about our Lord or of me his prisoner. Rather, join with me in suffering for the gospel, by the power of God.

1 John 5:9-11 We accept human testimony, but God's testimony is greater because it is the testimony of God, which he has given about his Son. 10 Whoever believes in the Son of God accepts this testimony. Whoever does not believe God has made him out to be a liar, because they have not believed the testimony God has given about his Son. 11 And this is the testimony: God has given us eternal life, and this life is in his Son.

Revelation 1:9 I, John, your brother and companion in the suffering and kingdom and patient endurance that are ours in Jesus, was on the island of Patmos because of the word of God and the testimony of Jesus.

Revelation 12:11 They triumphed over him by the blood of the Lamb and by the word of their testimony; they did not love their lives so much as to shrink from death.

Revelation 12:17 Then the dragon was enraged at the woman and went off to wage war against the rest of her offspring—those who keep God's commands and hold fast their testimony about Jesus.

Revelation 19:10 At this I fell at his feet to worship him. But he said to me, "Don't do that! I am a fellow servant with you and with your brothers and sisters who hold to the testimony of Jesus. Worship God! For it is the Spirit of prophecy who bears testimony to Jesus."

Revelation 20:4 I saw thrones on which were seated those who had been given authority to judge. And I saw the souls of those who had been beheaded because of their testimony about Jesus and because of the word of God. They had not worshiped the beast or its image and had not received its mark on their foreheads or their hands. They came to life and reigned with Christ a thousand years.

Can someone get saved on their deathbed?

I believe many people have gotten saved on their deathbeds. <u>Works aren't necessary for salvation, but are evidence that you *are* saved if you remain on this earth.</u>

Can someone be saved and not know it?

According to Carlton Pearson and others in the Universal Reconciliation movement, yes.

Yet, as I read the words of Jesus on faith, I don't think one can be oblivious to God, a hater of God, or devoted to evil—yet somehow be "unconsciously" saved.

Faith is *required* for salvation, and that means a *consciousness* of God

Faith involves a recognition of our need for Him, a willingness to drop the broken shards of our own lives, and receive His gift. The Bible speaks of the redeemed as those who have humbly sought God's promise (recognizing they cannot save or fix themselves).

> **Mark 10:15** [Jesus speaking] "Truly I tell you, anyone who will not receive the kingdom of God like a little child will never enter it." (The same statement is also found in Luke 18:17)

Receiving is directly connected to "believing" (faith).

> **John 1:11-13** He came to that which was his own, but his own did not receive him. 12 Yet to all who did receive him, to those who believed in his name, he gave the right to become children of God—13 children born not of natural descent, nor of human decision or a husband's will, but born of God.

Just a few weeks before I was ready to publish this book, I was in a Bible study with one of my pastors, Mickie Norman, and I was touched anew with Jesus' desire for us to actively seek Him out—and His promise that He won't disappoint anyone who does so. In one of the most famous passages of Scripture, *the Beatitudes*, Jesus said this:

> **Matthew 5:3-6** Blessed are the poor in spirit: for theirs is the kingdom of heaven.
> 4 Blessed are they that mourn: for they shall be comforted.
> 5 Blessed are the meek: for they shall inherit the earth.
> **6 Blessed are they which do hunger and thirst after righteousness: <u>for they shall be filled.</u>**—KJV

Jesus wants us to recognize our complete spiritual poverty—our *lostness*. He wants us to hunger and thirst for what He alone can offer. When we do, He promises us that we shall be filled.

Another metaphor (of many that could be made) is *Light and Revelation.*

Simeon, who had been promised by God that he wouldn't die before seeing the Messiah, saw the promise fulfilled.

> **Luke 2:28-32** Simeon took him in his arms and praised God, saying: 29 "Sovereign Lord, as you have promised, you may now dismiss your servant in peace. 30 For my eyes have seen your salvation, 31 which you have prepared in the sight of all nations: 32 a light for revelation to the Gentiles, and the glory of your people Israel."

By definition, "a revelation" means something is exposed or disclosed (and possibly shocks or surprises us)—but it's a revelation because we *see and apprehend* it. We are enlightened. While there are those who (like the tax collector in Luke 18:9-14) don't know a *formula* for salvation, there is still the revelation that God is holy, that they have fallen short, and that their highest longing is to be with Him. Such are those whom God will find a means to further reveal Himself (as He did with Cornelius in Acts 8). Are YOU the means by which God is trying to reach someone? Or are you a clanging gong with lots of words and no true love? Or are you just passing through, unconcerned about whether or not people know Jesus, thinking it's all good eventually?

Can people be reconciled to God *after* death?

The Christian Universalist Association says on their website that "souls" who leave this life "without significant spiritual growth will have other opportunities for learning after death" and they list 1 Pet. 3:18-20, 4:6. [lxvi]

Again, in the Bible, salvation is inseparably linked with the (physical) life that people have here on this earth. It is also contrary to the whole message of Jesus to say that salvation is the result of mere knowledge or "spiritual" growth. The Universalist idea that the people in Hell *are* "saved" but just not yet refined and educated enough (yet) for Heaven may have appeal, but either you belong to Jesus or you don't—there aren't *shades* of saved. A change of mind *after* you're in the grave would no longer accepting Christ through *faith*, it' would be a recognition of the undeniable.

But here are the Scriptures which The CUA listed as proof texts for their idea that there will be unlimited opportunities for "spiritual growth" and reconciliation with God after death:

> **1 Peter 3:18-20** For Christ also suffered once for sins, the righteous for the unrighteous, to bring you to God. He was put to death in the body but made alive in the Spirit. 19 After being made alive, he went and made proclamation to the imprisoned spirits — 20 to those who were disobedient long ago when God waited patiently in the days of Noah while the ark was being built. In it only a few people, eight in all, were saved through water . . .

Bible scholars find the above to be one of the "most difficult" passages in the New Testament to sort out. It's one of those passages that the original audience may have completely understood but no one today can say with *certainty* what it means. This fact alone makes the passage an easy opening for ideas *supplied by others* to be inserted and read *into* the text.

But, in context, is that what is Peter was saying? Let me add the rest of the sentence [that the CUA didn't include] to help clarify his meaning:

> **1 Peter 3:21** ". . . and this water symbolizes baptism that now saves you also—not the removal of dirt from the body but the pledge of a clear conscience toward God."

I submit that the main points of Peter's words were *Jesus,* the *water*, and *our pledge of faith.* It's demonstrating the connection between those Noah's day who believed God and were brought through the flood, and those who believe Jesus and are baptized as an act of faith in Him.

Any speculations regarding these verses are simply that—*speculations.* Like other ideas that hang upon the *possible* definition of a *single* word, I believe it's irresponsible to present the above as "Scriptural proof" of the CUA's speculations.

Here is the next verse they list as proof as post-death opportunities:

---

lxvi From the page *Universal Salvation* linked to the "Statement of Faith" page on the website for The Christian Universalist Assoc. http://www.christianuniversalist.org/articles/justice-afterlife.html (13 October 2011)

> **1 Peter 4:6** For this is the reason the gospel was preached even to those who are now dead, so that they might be judged according to human standards in regard to the body, but live according to God in regard to the spirit.

As a stand-alone verse, it might sound as if they are right. But let's add context here. Peter is encouraging people to live in *faith*, not in their former (sinful) manner. He is saying that their old, worldly friends will find it odd that they no longer partake of such things. Let's read it in the Amplified Version.

> **1 Peter 4:4-6** They are astonished and think it very queer that you do not now run hand in hand with them in the same excesses of dissipation, and they abuse [you]. 5 But they will have to give an account to Him Who is ready to judge and pass sentence on the living and the dead. **6 For this is why the good news (the Gospel) was preached [in their lifetime] even to the dead, that though judged in fleshly bodies as men are, they might live in the spirit as God does.**—Amplified Bible, words in parentheses and brackets are in the text, not added by me.

I admit it's a case of HOW you want to read vs. 6, but given the complete lack of mention of "multiple opportunities" after death in the Gospels or anywhere else in the New Testament, and the *large amount of Scriptures that contradict their interpretation*, I would say that this is something Universalists merely WISH was true.

The CUA then goes on to state that nobody (not even evil beings) can run out of chances to "return home to their Creator," and they list Ephesians 4:10 and Philippians 2:10, stating that this (idea of unlimited chances) is "God's promise!"[lxvii] Here is the text of the verses they list:

> **Ephesians 4:10** He who descended is the very one who ascended higher than all the heavens, in order to fill the whole universe.

> **Philippians 2:10** . . . that at the name of Jesus every knee should bow, in heaven and on earth and under the earth.

I think they probably intended to include more verses in each of these (which would have helped make their point in some measure), but even then it's a case of lifting something from the whole of the Bible and reading INTO it that which you want to see.

I would also add that mere *recognition* of God does not save:

> **James 2:19** You say you have faith, for you believe that there is one God. Good for you! <u>Even the demons believe this, and they tremble in terror.</u> —NLT

The Bible says that ALL people will be "resurrected" but what does that mean?

The Bible says that Jesus was the *first* resurrected being. (Ac 26:23; Col. 1:18, Rev 1:5) He rose from the grave with an immortal body and He is the only one with an immortal, resurrected body right now.

The term "resurrection" although it can apply to someone being resuscitated (in a body that will still age and perish, such as Lazarus in John 11), when it is applied to the future of humanity refers to the event when each soul will:

---

lxvii From the Universal Salvation page of the Christian Universalist Assoc. website http://www.christianuniversalist.org/articles/universalsalvation.html (16 Feb. 2012)

A. Receive a new, imperishable body like Jesus already has [eternal life] **OR**,

B. When the soul will be brought to life in order to stand before the Lord for judgment [condemnation—see the following page].

The term "soul" used here is a reference to the personality, will, mind desire, and awareness of a person (what makes you you) that exists beyond the death of the body.[lxviii]

The Two Groups of People Who are Resurrected in The New Testament

The resurrection called the "first" one is for people who are described as those who "believed" in Jesus as their Savior, those who belong to Him, who have longed to see Him. They are the ones whom Jesus will collect at His coming and who will be given imperishable bodies like His (John 10:25-26, Romans 8:29; Colossians 3:4, 1 Corinthians 15:20-49, 2 Timothy 4:8, Philippians 3:21, 2 Peter 1:4, 1 John 3:1-2, Revelation 20:5-6.) Jesus says that those who have heard His message and believed won't be "condemned" (John 5:24).

As referenced in Chapter 5, Jesus describes the resurrection of two groups of people in John 5:28-29 saying the first is for those being raised to "life" who "won't be condemned" and the second for those who *will* be condemned.

> **John 5:24-25** "Very truly I tell you, whoever hears my word and believes him who sent me has eternal life and will not be judged but has crossed over from death to life. 25 Very truly I tell you, a time is coming and has now come when the dead will hear the voice of the Son of God and those who hear will live."

> **John 5:28-29** "Do not be amazed at this, for a time is coming when all who are in their graves will hear his voice and come out—those who have done what is good will rise to live, and those who have done what is evil will rise to be condemned." (See also Matt. 25:46)

In Revelation 20:11-15, describes the next resurrection as "a thousand years" after the first one (whether you want to think of the time frame as symbolic or literal, it is describe as a *second* event) and that's when everyone else will be raised for judgment. There are no other resurrections mentioned. So when and where does this endless opportunity to be reconciled (made right) with God begin? When are these people resurrected and welcomed to Heaven? While Universalists might be able to read "reconciliation after death" into select (and I might add, abstract) verses, there are no clear references to it.

When would the "chastisement" phase of Hell take place? Do Universalists think it is when these people are disembodied souls in Hell until the thousand years is over? I see no verses about Jesus repeatedly trolling through Hell for those who have repented. Nor do I see any account of saints going to preach there. Nor is there a way given for them to graduate from Hell to Heaven when they repent sufficiently.

> **John 15:5** [Jesus speaking] "I am the vine; you are the branches. *If you remain in me* and I in you, you will bear much fruit; apart from me you can do nothing. This is to my Father's glory, that you bear much fruit, *showing* yourselves to be my disciples."

[lxviii] See Matt. 10:28, Matt. 22:37, 2 Cor. 5:8, Rev. 6:9, Rev. 20:4

View the above with other verses where Jesus says, "you fed me, you visited me, etc." or "anyone who denies me," etc.—ALL of which connect faith to physical bodies.

Or, do Universalists think that those who have rejected Christ throughout life are going to be raised again in *mortal* bodies for a season of chastening and repentance? If so, we have the problem of saying there is reincarnation—and the Bible speaks against such an idea.

Hebrews 9:27-28 Just as people are destined to die once, and after that to face judgment, so Christ was sacrificed once to take away the sins of many; and he will appear a second time, not to bear sin, but to bring salvation to those who are waiting for him.

Psalms 78:38-39 [speaking of God] Yet he was merciful; he forgave their iniquities and did not destroy them. Time after time he restrained his anger and did not stir up his full wrath. He remembered that they were but flesh, a passing breeze that does not return.

Or, do Universalists think that those who have rejected Christ throughout life are going to be raised in *imperishable* bodies for their season of chastening? But the Lord barred Adam and Eve from the garden to keep them from eating from the tree of life while in their sinful state.

No matter which Hell-as-Purgatory scenario they pick, it encounters significant scriptural obstacles. In addition, we have some Universalists saying people will have "endless" or "unlimited" chances to repent in this season of "intense chastening" after death. And, in my dictionary, the words "endless" and "unlimited" are in the definition of *eternal*. Universalists can't have it both ways (declaring that punishment *isn't* eternal but that intense chastening can be endless.)

The importance of sharing the Gospel of Jesus Christ (in deed _and_ word) during this lifetime

God wants people to repent while they're here—because *this life* IS our opportunity.

Luke 12:9 [Jesus speaking] "But anyone who denies me *here on earth* will be denied before God's angels." —NLT

Luke 13:1-5 Now there were some present at that time who told Jesus about the Galileans whose blood Pilate had mixed with their sacrifices. 2 Jesus answered, "Do you think that these Galileans were worse sinners than all the other Galileans because they suffered this way? 3 I tell you, no! But unless you repent, you too will all perish. 4 Or those eighteen who died when the tower in Siloam fell on them—do you think they were more guilty than all the others living in Jerusalem? 5 I tell you, no! But unless you repent, you too will all perish."

2 Peter 3:3-8 Above all, you must understand that in the last days scoffers will come, scoffing and following their own evil desires. 4 They will say, "Where is this 'coming' he promised? Ever since our ancestors died, everything goes on as it has since the beginning of creation." 5 But they deliberately forget that long ago by God's word the heavens came into being and the earth was formed out of water and by water. 6 By these waters also the world of that time was deluged and destroyed. 7 By the same word the present heavens and earth are reserved for fire, being kept for the day of judgment and destruction of the ungodly. 8 But do not forget this one thing, dear friends: With the Lord a day is like a thousand years, and a thousand years are like a day. 9 The Lord is not slow in keeping his promise, as some understand slowness. Instead he is patient with you, not wanting anyone to perish, but everyone to come to repentance.

TODAY is the day that counts

> Hebrews 3:12 See to it, brothers and sisters, that none of you has a sinful, unbelieving heart that turns away from the living God. 13 <u>But encourage one another daily, as long as it is called "Today," so that none of you may be hardened by sin's deceitfulness. 14 We have come to share in Christ, if indeed we hold our original conviction firmly to the very end.</u> 15 As has just been said:

> "Today, if you hear his voice, do not harden your hearts as you did in the rebellion."

> 16 Who were they who heard and rebelled? Were they not all those Moses led out of Egypt? 17 And with whom was he angry for forty years? Was it not with those who sinned, whose bodies perished in the wilderness? 18 And to whom did God swear that they would never enter his rest if not to those who disobeyed? 19 So we see that they were not able to enter, because of their unbelief.

The discipline/teaching of the Lord is for NOW

> Titus 2:11 For the grace of God has appeared that *offers* salvation to all people. 12 It <u>teaches</u> us to say "No" to ungodliness and worldly passions, and to live self-controlled, upright and godly lives <u>in this present age, 13 while we wait for the blessed hope</u>—the appearing of the glory of our great God and Savior, Jesus Christ, 14 who gave himself for us to redeem us from all wickedness and to purify for himself a people that are his very own, eager to do what is good.

In the books of Matthew, Mark, Luke, and John, we have the story of Jesus' life, words, and ministry from different perspectives. At the end of each of these books, Jesus has died and been resurrected. The book of Acts is sometimes called the "gospel of the Holy Spirit" because it is an account of what happened next—how the Holy Spirit filled, equipped, and guided the Church and how early Christians lived.

A Quote from Mother Theresa

Some have said that, after Jesus was resurrected, everything was "done" and now all people would be (or eventually are) saved. They say that there is now no reason to make a case or a plea for salvation. I know that I'm about to tip a sacred cow, *but here goes!*—Although few in the history of the world could match the charitable works of Mother Theresa, I'm saddened by her famous quote that people use to promote the "no need to share the gospel" idea:

> "There is only one God and He is God to all; therefore it is important that everyone is seen as equal before God. I've always said we should help a Hindu become a better Hindu, a Muslim become a better Muslim, a Catholic become a better Catholic."[lxix]

In part, I agree with Mother Theresa. There is only one God (and whether or not someone else recognizes this, it doesn't diminish the fact that God is God). I also acknowledge that all people are created in His image, and are worthy of our respect. HOWEVER I strongly disagree with the thought that we as Christians are simply called to make *anyone* "better" at believing or practicing falsehood.

[lxix] ETWN the Global Catholic Network http://www.ewtn.com/motherteresa/words.htm (May 13, 2012)

New Testament examples of God's love for people and His desire to set them free

In Chapter 2 of this book I shared about a meeting Jesus had with a Samaritan woman. Suffice to say, that Jesus didn't give her false beliefs *any* endorsement. He wanted to lead her to the truth about the Messiah and true worship.

In Acts 8 (vs. 4-29) we see Philip in Samaria. The people in this place were following a man by the name of Simon and calling him "the Great Power of God." Philip doesn't just blend in and "help" people become better followers of Simon, he boldly proclaims the Kingdom of God and Gospel of Jesus Christ and there are miracles that amaze even Simon the sorcerer. According to Scripture many believed and were baptized—even Simon.

Shortly thereafter, Peter and other apostles arrive to impart the baptism of the Holy Spirit but there is a problem. Simon asks to "buy" the Holy Spirit so that he can lay hands on people and impart the Spirit to them. Did Peter just assume it was ignorance on the part of Simon and pray for the man to receive the gift of the Spirit anyway? No. Does he take Simon aside and say, "Hey brother, you're mistaken about this . . ."? No. Peter discerns that something is totally amok in Simon, that the man is "captive to sin" and full of bitterness. Peter says he's not even sure that Simon can be forgiven for his evil intentions! If you read the passage, Simon doesn't *ask* for forgiveness, either (and there are some historical accounts that say Simon went on to lead a totally blasphemous, idolatrous, sinful life). There are several theological debates (other than those about Universalism) that could be had at this point—but what I want you to note here is that <u>Peter the apostle</u> believed the man to be "*captive*" (in bondage) to sin, and he wasn't even sure the man could be forgiven for the evil intent of his heart! It is my own belief that *if* Simon had repented, God would have forgiven him, but (taken with Jesus' comments about blasphemy against the Holy Spirit—Matthew 12:32, Mark 3:29, Luke 12:10) it certainly makes a case that there are some who are *not* forgiven (if for no other reason than that they are so hard-hearted they *refuse* to repent and receive forgiveness).

After this (still in Acts 8) Philip is sent by the Lord to a road where he meets an Ethiopian eunuch. Much like the Samaritan woman that Jesus met, the eunuch was someone who would *never* have been considered clean enough for the inner courts of the temple in Jerusalem. There was no work or ceremony within the law that could make him completely acceptable. However, Philip shares the Gospel message of Jesus with the eunuch and even baptizes him. The eunuch was accepted into the Body of Christ. Please note, the elements of the story: The gospel was explained, the eunuch made a decision/request, and it was granted.

In Acts 10 we see that an angel of God appeared to a man by the name of Cornelius—an officer in the Roman army. This wasn't a random event on the Lord's part. Cornelius had been seeking God with prayer and fasting. And, in fact, his prayers had been heard by Jehovah God. But was that enough? Was the angel sent to tell Cornelius he needed to do nothing else, that he'd found the way and everything was fine? No. The angel told Cornelius to send for Peter.

Now, as a Jew, Peter would have thought going to the house of Cornelius was absolutely wrong, but God told him not to consider "something unclean if God has made it clean." Is this a statement saying everyone was now onboard the S.S. Salvation? Context says no. If you read the whole story, you will see that God IS telling Peter to have respect for ALL people—but the unsaved STILL need to be saved. Let's look.

Peter went to the house of Cornelius and by the time Peter got to the soldier's house, it was filled with all sorts of Gentiles. Let's see what Peter did next.

Acts 10:28-29 Peter told them, "You know it is against our laws for a Jewish man to enter a Gentile home like this or to associate with you. But God has shown me that I should no longer think of anyone as impure or unclean. 29 So I came without objection as soon as I was sent for. Now tell me why you sent for me." —NLT

Cornelius tells Peter about the angel visitation. Does Peter say . . . "Well then, what do you need ME for? You got it already!" ???? No! PETER UNDERSTANDS THAT GOD IS SAYING ANYONE CAN BE SAVED, THAT THE WHOLE WORLD IS A HARVEST FIELD.

Acts 10:34-36, 42-43 Opening his mouth, Peter said:

"I most certainly understand now that <u>God is not one to show partiality, *35 but in every nation the man who fears Him and does what is right is welcome to Him*</u>. 36 The word which He sent to the sons of Israel, preaching peace through Jesus Christ (He is Lord of all) . . . . 42 And He ordered us to preach to the people, and solemnly to testify that this is the One who has been appointed by God as Judge of the living and the dead. 43 <u>Of Him all the prophets bear witness that through His name everyone who believes in Him receives forgiveness of sins</u>."—NASB

It was Father God who led Jesus and the people of the early church to those who were already seeking Him in some fashion, but not in full possession of what was necessary to have open access to the courts of Father God in the Kingdom of Heaven. Is there evidence in *any* of these cases (or in the travels of Paul), that they just tried to help people to be *better* idol worshippers, or *better* intellectuals, or *better* sorcerers? No. God DOES meet people "where they're at," but He wants to bring them to something better! For Philip, or Peter, or Paul or anyone in the church—to not share the gospel would have been to deny what they were called to do.

In Acts 26, Paul is giving his testimony (of his conversion and his call to go out and preach the message of Christ) to Festus and King Agrippa.

"One day I was on such a mission to Damascus, armed with the authority and commission of the leading priests. 13 About noon, Your Majesty, as I was on the road, a light from heaven brighter than the sun shone down on me and my companions. 14 We all fell down, and I heard a voice saying to me in Aramaic, 'Saul, Saul, why are you persecuting me? It is useless for you to fight against my will.'

15 "'Who are you, lord?' I asked.

"And the Lord replied, 'I am Jesus, the one you are persecuting. 16 Now get to your feet! For I have appeared to you to appoint you as my servant and witness. You are to tell the world what you have seen and what I will show you in the future. 17 And I will rescue you from both your own people and the Gentiles. <u>Yes, I am sending you to the Gentiles 18 to open their eyes, so they may turn from darkness to light and from the power of Satan to God. Then they will receive forgiveness for their sins and be given a place among God's people, who are set apart by faith in me.</u>'

19 "And so, King Agrippa, I obeyed that vision from heaven. 20 I preached first to those in Damascus, then in Jerusalem and throughout all Judea, and also to the Gentiles, <u>that all must repent of their sins and turn to God</u>—and prove they have changed by the good things they do." Acts 26: 12-20—NLT

Boundaries? In the "Age of Grace" we don't need no stinkin' boundaries! . . . Or do we?

I have a brother in the Lord (and you know who you are Jim Wehde) who is a surveyor by trade. He travels quite a bit surveying land for malls, corporations, perspective buyers, etc. Sometimes he's in the city, sometimes in the wilderness, but his job is to accurately mark the boundaries of parcels of land. Sometimes, I'm sure part of his job is to help settle disputes over who owns what. It brings order to chaos.

But, in matters of faith, why have boundaries? Doesn't that just create a mentality that says some "have it" and some don't? Doesn't it give some of those who think they "have it" a superior attitude? Doesn't it make some actively seek to "exclude" others? To that I can only say that if someone or even a whole church has an attitude problem, they aren't following Christ.

The Church didn't create a boundary between man and God, nor are we responsible for maintaining it. It was established *by God* the day that Adam and Eve were expelled from the place where they had once walked and talked with Him in open communion.

In John 3:17-18 (these are the next lines *after* the most famous Bible verse). Jesus says,

> "For God did not send his Son into the world to condemn the world, but to save the world through him. Whoever believes in him is not condemned, but whoever does not believe stands condemned already . . ."

The "prince of this world," (Satan) and the world itself—its ways, means, systems, powers, and everything that would *belong* to this world (via the fall of mankind)—stood condemned on the day Adam and Eve were expelled from the garden. All of these things were and are on a collision course with destruction. The "natural" course of this world is dragged (yes dragged) along under the power of darkness. The Good News is that Jesus has made a way for us to become citizens of the kingdom of God so that we can choose to no longer *belong* to this world.

John 10:27 My sheep hear My voice, and I know them, and they follow Me.—NASB

John 16:7-11 [Jesus speaking] But very truly I tell you, it is for your good that I am going away. Unless I go away, the Advocate will not come to you; but if I go, I will send him to you. 8 When he comes, he will prove the world to be in the wrong about sin and righteousness and judgment: 9 about sin, because people do not believe in me; 10 about righteousness, because I am going to the Father, where you can see me no longer; 11 and about judgment, because the prince of this world now stands condemned. The Holy Spirit (the Advocate) is the one who will convince the world of sin and of the judgment that has *already been decreed* against it—and the world will always be at enmity with the Kingdom of light.

John 15:9 The world would love you as one of its own if you belonged to it, *but you are no longer part of the world.* I chose you to come out of the world, so it hates you.

John 17:14-16 [Jesus praying to Father] "I have given them Your word; and the world has hated them, because they are not of the world, even as I am not of the world. 15 I do not ask You to take them out of the world, but to keep them from the evil one. 16 They are not of the world, even as I am not of the world."—NASB

What IF . . .

. . . we just turn the boundary thing on its end for a moment and look at it from a different light?

Suppose you were born in the grips of some horrible dictatorship that had stolen everything from you, and killed your family. For years, you have wanted to escape. Despite constant loudspeaker bombardment telling you that you are in a happy place, that you should rejoice (under pain of death), and that everyone else here is grateful to the fearless leader . . . you know you're not. You *know* you don't belong here. For long days and nights you seek, travel, sleep in wild woods, go hungry, go thirsty . . . all in search of escape. Since you've never experienced true freedom, you're not sure what all it entails, but you *know* that you want it. And then, one day you see it: a city on a hill, filled with light.

How would you feel when you stepped across the boundary to that kingdom?

There are literally millions of people who struggle and suffer under the weight of sin and sorrow every day, *and I myself was one of them*. I searched for something that would free my soul, but always had this nagging, fearful "knowing" inside me that my life was spinning out of my control . . . and my steering wheel and brakes were broken! How I longed for peace, safety, and love. No televangelist had to tell me my life was a wreck in progress—I knew it already.

Oh the JOY that came to me the night I took the hand that was offered to me and stepped into the Kingdom of Heaven! Oh the deliverance and the peace that flooded into to me!

Jesus wasn't the one who had kept me in the dark. Jesus wasn't rejoicing over the horrors of my life—He was a shining gateway to freedom. So how is it *unfair* that His light shined in the darkness exposing my need?

The world is *already* in the grip of darkness and death. According to Jesus, the world is already condemned[lxx] so it's not my "job" to condemn the world, I'm supposed to be showing the way to escape it.

Are we "keepin' it real" or just makin' it weird? Are Christian leaders and teachers called to become part of the world's system in order to stay relevant?

Seeking to wrap the Gospel around the ideas of inclusiveness and diversity, the "love" of Universalism/Universal Reconciliation allows people to sidestep the first commandment (loving the Lord first and foremost) and skip right to the world's version of "love thy neighbor" which, in this do-your-own-thing society is (at best) a *philanthropic love. It's the kind of thing that wins the recognition and praise of the world—because it requires no change of the status quo.*

But we all need to remember the reason they crucified Jesus wasn't that He loved people or because He did good works—they killed Him because He claimed to be equal (in every way) to Father God and He asked people to believe this, to deny themselves, and follow Him. It wasn't merely the Sanhedrin or the Pharisees or the ruling Roman government who hated Jesus, it was the world—because Jesus required change of all of them. The same is true today.

> **Matthew 10:22** [Jesus speaking] "You will be hated by everyone *because of me*, but the one who stands firm to the end will be saved."
>
> **Luke 6:22** [Jesus speaking] "Blessed are you when people hate you, when they exclude you and insult you and reject your name as evil, *because of the Son of Man*."
>
> **Luke 21:17** [Jesus speaking] "Everyone will hate you *because of me*."
>
> **John 15:18-19** [Jesus speaking] "If the world hates you, keep in mind that it hated me first. 19 *If you belonged to the world*, it would love you as its own. As it is, you do not belong to the world, but I have chosen you out of the world. That is why the world hates you."

[lxx] John 3:17-20, John 16:1-11

Author of *The Jesus Style*, Gayle Erwin, wryly says those verses aren't the kind you find in Scripture promise boxes. :-)

> Know this: If the world can't praise you enough, it's generally not a good sign.

The *world* says you should strive to be liked by all 1,852 of your cyber friends, but you know what? If you walk with Jesus, the scrape of it against the world's slimy surface is going to happen. Please know that I'm not talking about Christians having a martyr attitude, or operating in a religious spirit, or using the law like a weapon on people. I'm talking about each of us living life as a follower of Jesus Christ, and when given the opportunity, sharing about Him and what He accomplished on the cross. He asks us to live, for our part, at peace with all—but we are called to serve as ambassadors of Truth and Light in a place filled with darkness and lies. Don't say Jesus didn't warn ye.

The World's Infatuation with the Walking Dead

What if Satan could just come up with a marketing plan to make *staying dead* more appealing?

Great Marketing = The world's fascination with the walking dead—
Zombies and werewolves and vampires, oh my!

The world has fallen in love with Death. And even if you're not a fan of Death, there is a default option that Satan HOPES you'll take: Passivity. While I'm sure he'd love to have you bow before him, it's not necessary. You're a citizen of his realm until you CHOOSE another citizenship.

Yet Satan has done this *brilliant* marketing thing. I mean, honestly, if your kingdom consists of darkness, sorrow, pain, sickness, suffering, and death . . . how do you get your slaves to stay when they find out they can escape? You plot and plan until you get this fantabulous idea: Why not frame it all in the opposite? Why not make a living death <u>appealing</u>?

Let's see now . . . what would a majority of people still classify as a sinful thing? How about being a serial killer? So . . . let's see. How about if we write lots of books and TV shows and movies about serial killers—and make them powerful, sexy heroes. Like vampires. Or werewolves. People who live on and on, but suffer from a curse from which they cannot free themselves. Part of the story depicts how they continually hunger and thirst in a way that will *never* be satisfied—but they're cool. Of course, in order to placate viewers and fans who want a "moral message," we'll make it plain that we should only love the "good" serial killer heroes, not their evil serial killer enemies. And in the TV and movie versions these characters (who are forever separated from light) can even wear pale makeup that makes them look sick/dead and it will be all the rage! The world will *want* to delve into the dark and be like them! . . . And we can even sell dolls that look like this to children . . . and make cartoon versions of adorable *little* serial killers. . . . Oh wait. Hasn't someone already done that?

Jesus: "Come to me, you who are heavy laden, and I will give you rest."

Satan: "WHAT? Listen folks, he's calling you lazy! He's sayin' you can't pull yourselves up by your own bootstraps! He doesn't want you to have it YOUR way!"

Jesus: "I am the Living Water. Whoever drinks the water I give them will never thirst. Indeed, the water I give them will become in them a spring of water welling up to eternal life."

Satan: "Uhhhh . . . I have organic *piña coladas* here! Or strawberry power drinks with only 2 net carbs! Think about it guys. Water is so . . . boring."

Jesus: "I came to set captives free. I came to open the prison doors."

Satan: "WHAT? Now he's calling you 'slaves' and 'inmates' folks. What an insult! You're not in bondage, you're just really *into* things."

Jesus: "Listen to me and walk with me now."

Satan: "Now schmow. If Jesus *really* created time, he'll give you *plenty* of time. If it's absolutely necessary, you can always do it later."

Jesus: "Truly I tell you, unless someone becomes like little child, they will never enter the kingdom of heaven."

Satan: "Are you saying you want my friends here to be *immature*? And—*AHA!*—Did I hear a condition to enter your kingdom? Whatever happened to unconditional love? Listen to ME, people, this guy is an imposter! The *real* Jesus would love you just as you are—so don't go changing a thing. Trust me! I know what I'm talking about! It's in Matthew 37:6!"

You name <u>anything</u> that represents darkness or evil and there is some organization, publisher, producer, writer, network, or popular personality who gets inspired to market it and make it appealing. . . . And even when people become aware of true darkness, Satan will use all the means at his disposal to make offering an escape from it seem as pointless as wearing sunscreen in a cave or as heartless as giving peanut brittle to a man with no teeth. The devil can't really keep people in his realm, so he has to make them *want* to stay or make them believe escape is dumb, unnecessary . . . or impossible.

What each of us has to decide is: Who is telling us the truth? Is it the temporary ruler of this world system (who gleefully rides over all this devastation, sorrow, sickness, and death) who says you can always do something now and apologize or pay for it (if necessary) *later*? OR is the one telling the truth Jesus—the One who left all the glories of Heaven to come down here and give up His very life in order to become your doorway of escape *right now*?

God sent Adam and Eve from the garden and blocked the entrance at that time because He didn't want them to eat of the tree of Life and live eternally in their fallen state (there will be no zombies in paradise!) A boundary was set, the entrance blocked *at God's command*. To open the way to LIFE again, God gave up His one and only Son to pay the ransom for us. He opens a door we must CHOOSE to walk through, a WAY we must choose to take, Living Water we must choose to drink, spiritual food we must choose to eat, a GIFT we must choose to receive and open—*in this life*.

In the final words of his gospel, in order to sum up the purpose of what he'd written, John the apostle wrote the following:

> **John 20:30-31** Jesus performed many other signs in the presence of his disciples, which are not recorded in this book. *But these are written that you may believe that Jesus is the Messiah, the Son of God, and that by believing you may have life in his name.*

In a letter he also wrote:

> **1 John 5:6-12** And Jesus Christ was revealed as God's Son by his baptism in water and by shedding his blood on the cross—not by water only, but by water and blood. And the Spirit, who is truth, confirms it with his testimony. 7 So we have these three witnesses—8 the Spirit, the water, and the blood—and all three agree. 9 Since we believe human testimony, surely we

can believe the greater testimony that comes from God. And God has testified about his Son. 10 All who believe in the Son of God know in their hearts that this testimony is true. Those who don't believe this are actually calling God a liar because they don't believe what God has testified about his Son.

11 *And this is what God has testified: He has given us eternal life, and this life is in his Son. 12 Whoever has the Son has life; whoever does not have God's Son does not have life.*

This tells me that *God*, not man, has established a border—so that when you cross it, you know you are saved. Here it is in the next sentence of the passage:

1 John 5:13 I have written this to you who believe in the name of the Son of God, so that you may know you have eternal life.

Here is a list of New Testament Scriptures I have collected over time that connect salvation to personal FAITH (this is stated not only in the individual verses, but in context as well). I intentionally put them in a single column so you have room for your own Scripture verses and notes.

Matthew 3:12
Matthew 5:18-26
Matthew 7:13-14
Matthew 12:10, 30-32
Matthew 12:46-50
Matthew 18:3, 8-9
Matthew 25:41
Matthew 28:18
Mark 3:42-48
Mark 9:42-48
Mark 9:47-48
Luke 2:14-30
Luke 3:17
Luke 8:20-21
Luke 9:23-24
Luke 13:3-5
Luke 15:24
John 1:7
John 1:12
John 3:1-18
John 3:36
John 4:24
John 5:24-30
John 6:29, 39-40
John 8:12, 23-24, 51
John 11:25-26, 40
John 14:6
John 15:6
John 17:1-9, 25-26
John 20:31

Acts 2:17-21, 36-39
Acts 3:16-20, 23
Acts 4:12
Acts 5:32
Acts 10:41-43
Acts 13:38-39, 46-51
Acts 15:7-14
Acts 16:25-34
Acts 24:24-26
Acts 26:17-18, 28-29
Romans 1:16-17
Romans 3 (especially vs. 9-30)
Romans 6:18-19
Romans 8:8-11
Romans 10:4, 9-10, 14-17
Romans 11:19-21
1 Corinthians 1:2
1Corinthians 2:9
1 Corinthians 2:14
1 Corinthians 6:9-10
1 Corinthians 5:5
1 Corinthians 7:12-16
2 Corinthians 5:17
2 Corinthians 7:10
Galatians 3:2, 8-9, 14, 26
Galatians 5:20-22
Ephesians 1:10-15
Ephesians 2:8-21
Ephesians 3:12
Ephesians 4:17:18
Philippians 1:27-30
Philippians 3:18-19
Colossians 1:5-6, 16-17, 20, 23, 28
Colossians 2:12
1 Thessalonians 2:13
1 Thessalonians 5:1-3
2 Thessalonians 1:5-9
1 Timothy 1:1, 16
1 Timothy 2:5
1 Timothy 6:9
2 Timothy 2:10-12, 18
2 Timothy 2:18
2 Timothy 3:2, 8, 15
2 Timothy 4:1, 8
Hebrews 4, 5, 6 (the whole chapters)
Hebrews 5:9
Hebrews 6:1
Hebrews 7:25

Hebrews 10:39
Hebrews 11:6
Hebrews 12:4
Hebrews 15:7-9
James 1:12
1 Peter 1:3-5, 9, 22
1 Peter 3:1-2
2 Peter 3:9
2 Peter 2:1-3
2 Peter 2:6-9
2 Peter 3:6-9
1 John 2:23-25
1 John 3:1, 8, 10
1 John 4:7
1 John 5:5-12
2 John 1:7-11
Jude 1:6-8
Revelation 2:6, 10, 13-16, 19, 26
Revelation 3:1-6, 8-11, 20
Revelation 14:9-11
Revelation 20:14-15
Revelation 21:1-8

CHAPTER 9—THE PARABLES

I know parables and symbolic speech are fertile ground for anyone with an imagination, so let me repeat something I said earlier. As with metaphors, we must realize that there is an ever-present temptation to make parables mean something more, less, or *other* than what God intended.

Again, I remind you that the Lord *did* use parables, but *didn't* contradict Himself. Jesus wasn't saying one thing in public (with a wink wink, nudge nudge), and then denying it all behind the scenes when He talked to the disciples. The "deeper" meaning of the parable wasn't a contradiction of the obvious meaning. God is not the author of confusion.

The parable of **the Unmerciful Servant** (Matthew 18:21-35) is used by Universalists to promote the idea of a temporary hell, of limited punishment for even those who would be considered the "worst" sinners. So let's consider it:

To the priests and elders Jesus tells this parable: A man is called to pay his debt to the King and begs for mercy. The king actually cancels the debt, but then the man unmercifully tries to collect a debt from someone else. The king then calls him back and has him thrown into prison until he pays his own (original) debt.

This would appear to at least give some wiggle room to Universalists in that IF we extrapolate further than the parable goes, we could say that the servant would somehow be allowed to "pay his debt" and be released from prison (which they believe corresponds to their version of a limited hell).

First of all . . . is it Biblical to say that any person can *ever* pay the debt of sin? No. I would suggest that the "prison" doesn't refer to Hell, but to the chastening *in this life* (consequences of our sin/unforgiveness) that hopefully leads us to repentance.

A bottom-line look at the parables that speak of "the end"

Let's look and see if there are any continuing threads of thought in the parables of Jesus regarding what comes after death or at the end. Is the repeated message of these parables one of endless chances, OR of grace offered NOW with the choice (and the consequences of it) being ours?

The Sower (Matthew 13:1-23)—The sower throws seeds *everywhere*, but several places (along the path, among the rocks, among the thorns) the seed thrown never bears fruit and there is nothing to harvest. The sower also throws seed in good ground where it produces fruit for the harvest. (Also found in Luke 8. Remember, according to Jesus, only those who "remain/abide" in Jesus—those who are His—bear good fruit.)

The tares (Matthew 13:24-30, 36-43)—An "enemy" sows weeds among the farmer's crop but the weeds are allowed to grow there. In the end, the weeds are pulled up, bound, and burned.

> [Jesus speaking] "The one who sowed the good seed is the Son of Man. 38 The field is the world, and the good seed stands for the people of the kingdom. The weeds are the *people* of the evil one, 39 and the enemy who sows them is the devil. The harvest is the end of the age, and the harvesters are angels."

40 "As the weeds are pulled up and burned in the fire, so it will be at the end of the age. 41 The Son of Man will send out his angels, and they will weed out of his kingdom everything that causes sin **and all who do evil**. 42 They will throw them into the blazing furnace, where there will be weeping and gnashing of teeth."

The drag net (Matthew 13:47-50)—this one is short, so I'll put the whole thing here (remember, Jesus is speaking)

"Once again, the kingdom of heaven is like a net that was let down into the lake and *caught all kinds of fish*. When it was full, the fishermen pulled it up on the shore. Then they sat down and collected the good fish in baskets, but threw the bad away. This is how it will be at the end of the age. The angels will come and separate the wicked from the righteous and throw them into the blazing furnace, where there will be weeping and gnashing of teeth."

The Lost Sheep (Matthew 18:10-14 and Luke 15:3-7)—Jesus says we must not despise these "little ones" (open to interpretation, but I believe there is a good case to say this refers to people who have come with child-like faith). The shepherd is willing to leave 99 of his sheep to go and find the one that is lost.

The Tenants (Matthew 21:33-44)—To the priests and elders, Jesus tells this parable: A landlord plants a vineyard, puts a wall around it with a watchtower, then rents it to tenants who then beat the rent collectors and eventually kill the landlord's son. Jesus asks what the landlord will do when he comes, then says,

"Therefore I tell you that *the kingdom of God will be taken away from you* and given to a people who will produce its fruit."

In all fairness, I believe this one speaks of what happened here on earth. The priests and elders (who presumed to have the keys to heaven) were removed by Jesus (whom they killed). If they repented I believe they were saved.

The great supper (Luke 14:15-24)—The master's servants are told to go and tell invited guests to come to a banquet. They all make excuses and don't come. The master tells his servants to *compel* people from highways, byways (everywhere) to come to the feast. The master finishes by saying, of those who refused at first, "I tell you, not one of those who were invited will get a taste of my banquet."

Hmmmmmmm. Wedding feast. Servants told to *go out everywhere and urgently ask* people to come to the feast. The ones who declined the invitation will never get into the banquet.

The laborers in the vineyard (Matthew 20:1-16, also in Mark 12:1-11)—The men who work all day are angry because those who worked in the last hour get the same wages.

Note there are no disputes about wages for people who didn't accept **the offer** to be hired or who did no work at all.

The pounds (Luke 19:11-27)—A man goes away to become a king and leaves servants with money to put to use until he gets back. Two servants do well, one buried his portion of the money and he says he did this because he knew the king was a "hard man" (my note: this point is important). The King is angry that the man dared to call him "hard" for expecting a return on his money, and says, "I will judge you by your own words, you wicked servant!" The king tells others to take that servant's money away, then goes on to say, "I tell you that to everyone who has, more will be given, but as for the one who has nothing, even what they have will be taken away." He brings up the subject of being made king and says, "But those enemies of mine who did not want me to be king over them—bring them here and kill them in front of me."

The evil sharecroppers (Matthew 21:33-44; Mark 12:1-12; Luke 20:9-18)—In all three versions, the owner comes and kills the evil sharecroppers.

The marriage of the king's son (Matthew 22:1-14)—This is similar to the parable of the great supper in Luke 14. The king sends for his guests but some ignore the invitation while others beat and killed the servants he sent. Jesus adds this ending:

> 7 "The king was furious, and he sent out his army to destroy the murderers and burn their town. 8 And he said to his servants, 'The wedding feast is ready, and the guests I invited aren't worthy of the honor. 9 <u>Now go out to the street corners and invite everyone you see.</u>' 10 <u>So the servants brought in everyone they could find, good and bad alike,</u> and the banquet hall was filled with guests.
>
> 11 "<u>But when the king came in to meet the guests, he noticed a man who wasn't wearing the proper clothes for a wedding. 12 'Friend,' he asked, 'how is it that you are here without wedding clothes?' But the man had no reply. 13 Then the king said to his aides, 'Bind his hands and feet and throw him into the outer darkness, where there will be weeping and gnashing of teeth."</u>—NASB

Ten virgins (Matthew 25:1-13)—All ten virgins think they are invited to the feast. Five don't have the oil to light their way in the dark when the bridegroom is coming and are told to go buy some for themselves. They show up later and bang on the door. The bridegroom says, "Truly I tell you, I don't know you."

The talents (Matthew 25:14-30)—This is similar to the parable of the pounds, except that Jesus adds this statement:

> "So take the bag of gold from him and give it to the one who has ten bags. 29 For whoever has will be given more, and they will have an abundance. Whoever does not have, even what they have will be taken from them. And throw that worthless servant outside, into the darkness, where there will be weeping and gnashing of teeth."

Warnings of Jesus with parables

> **Matthew 24:45-51** "Who then is the faithful and wise servant, whom the master has put in charge of the servants in his household to give them their food at the proper time? It will be good for that servant whose master finds him doing so when he returns. Truly I tell you, he will put him in charge of all his possessions. But suppose that servant is wicked and says to himself, 'My master is staying away a long time,' and he then begins to beat his fellow servants and to eat and drink with drunkards. The master of that servant will come on a day when he does not expect him and at an hour he is not aware of. He will cut him to pieces and assign him a place with the hypocrites, where there will be weeping and gnashing of teeth."
>
> **Matthew 25:31-46** "But when the Son of Man comes in His glory, and all the angels with Him, then He will sit on His glorious throne. 32 All the nations will be gathered before Him; and He will separate them from one another, as the shepherd separates the sheep from the goats; 33 and He will put the sheep on His right, and the goats on the left.
>
> 34 "Then the King will say to those on His right, 'Come, you who are blessed of My Father, inherit the kingdom prepared for you from the foundation of the world. 35 For I was hungry,

and you gave Me something to eat; I was thirsty, and you gave Me something to drink; I was a stranger, and you invited Me in; 36 naked, and you clothed Me; I was sick, and you visited Me; I was in prison, and you came to Me.' 37 Then the righteous will answer Him, 'Lord, when did we see You hungry, and feed You, or thirsty, and give You something to drink? 38 And when did we see You a stranger, and invite You in, or naked, and clothe You? 39 When did we see You sick, or in prison, and come to You?' 40 The King will answer and say to them, 'Truly I say to you, to the extent that you did it to one of these brothers of Mine, even the least of them, you did it to Me.'"

41 "Then He will also say to those on His left, ' Depart from Me, accursed ones, into the eternal fire which has been prepared for the devil and his angels; 42 for I was hungry, and you gave Me nothing to eat; I was thirsty, and you gave Me nothing to drink; 43 I was a stranger, and you did not invite Me in; naked, and you did not clothe Me; sick, and in prison, and you did not visit Me.' 44 Then they themselves also will answer, 'Lord, when did we see You hungry, or thirsty, or a stranger, or naked, or sick, or in prison, and did not take care of You?' 45 Then He will answer them, 'Truly I say to you, to the extent that you did not do it to one of the least of these, you did not do it to Me.' 46 These will go away into **eternal** punishment, but the righteous into **eternal** life."—NASB

(Emphasis on the word "eternal" in the verse above is mine. In both cases, the word in italics above is the Greek word *aionios*. It is used to apply to both punishment AND life.)

I find it hard to believe that all of these sayings (and more) are mere symbolism or zealous *exaggerations* on the part of Jesus.

Sobering Conclusion For This Chapter

Once again, I want you to ask yourself:

1. Did Jesus <u>ever</u> say something that was idle chatter?

2. Does Jesus Christ need to engage in empty threats to accomplish a goal?

3. Did Jesus ever tell a parable or story in public and then, in private, say it meant something totally opposite?

The answer to all of these questions is, "No." That means we must hear His words—not only on the great mercy, healing, and love He purchased for us but also the words on *what* He judges, *when* He judges, and *whom* He judges.

> Jesus had a LOT to say about judgment and punishment. I don't think He was doing so because He ran out of stuff to say and was just fond of hearing His own voice. He knew that it was important for us to realize there are consequences to what we choose.

CHAPTER 10—The BIG picture

Placing what Jesus *says* about loving the Father, discipleship, judgment, and punishment in the context of what He *does*.

On the Christian Universalist Association website, a link from their "What We Believe" page leads to another page which says, the "Golden Rule" (loving others) is "the most basic, essential moral teaching." They believe it's not coincidental that they find this rule in "many of the world's great religions and philosophies," and state that "All of true morality" comes from this "Golden Rule." [lxxi] Those in the CUA are not alone. Many Universalists have humanitarian love at the center of their work and teaching.

Humanitarian love driving us to acts of kindness may be admirable to the world, but if we are not guided by the Holy Spirit, to walk in the footsteps of Jesus, then it is of no eternal value.

One of the foundational errors of Universalism in my opinion is the (perhaps unintended) shift in focus from God (as the one whom all should seek while it is yet called "today") to this nebulous *Oh, you'll get the idea eventually* philosophy. While they happily quote slices of verses with Jesus' words on loving people . . . they are often missing the POINT of His reason for stepping into our timeline.

Who IS Jesus? Who did He say He was? Let's look at some of the names He chose for Himself: "The Door, The Way, The Truth, The Light, The Gate"

These are all the MEANS of finding access, of discernment, of determining which way to go. Jesus came and gave His life to give access to our Heavenly Father to **all people**—but He specifically stated that those who attempted to enter by other means were thieves and robbers who would be removed.

Jesus said that loving God was the greatest (most important) commandment.

Matthew 22:35-37 One of them, an expert in the law, tested him with this question: 36 "Teacher, which is the greatest commandment in the Law?"

37 Jesus replied: "'Love the Lord your God with all your heart and with all your soul and with all your mind.' 38 This is the first and greatest commandment. 39 And the second is like it: 'Love your neighbor as yourself.' 40 All the Law and the Prophets hang on these two commandments."

Here it is again in Mark's gospel.

Mark 12:28-31 One of the teachers of the law came and heard them debating. Noticing that Jesus had given them a good answer, he asked him, "Of all the commandments, which is the most important?"

29 "The most important one," answered Jesus, "is this: 'Hear, O Israel: The Lord our God, the Lord is one. 30 Love the Lord your God with all your heart and with all your soul and with all your mind and with all your strength.' 31 The second is this: 'Love your neighbor as yourself.' There is no commandment greater than these."

---

lxxi http://www.christianuniversalist.org/articles/goldenrule.html accessed 02/16/2912

Jesus' *whole life* is a testimony to the love of Father God. Everything in His life and ministry was rooted in giving Father God worship and the highest priority in His life and providing a means by which ANY person could enter into that same relationship. Yet, from the foundation up, much of Universalism sets acceptance of diversity and loving people as the highest model.

From the book of Genesis all the way to the book of Revelation the mandate given is to have faith in God and His promise. Faith is defined as a continued *abiding* in His promise (who, according the New Testament IS Christ). And "abiding" presumes a physical body (as in believing while we are *in this life*).

> **Matthew 10:38-39** "If you don't go all the way with me, through thick and thin, you don't deserve me. If your first concern is to look after yourself, you'll never find yourself. But if you forget about yourself and look to me, you'll find both yourself and me."—MSG

> **John 15:5-8** "I am the vine, you are the branches; he who abides in Me and I in him, he bears much fruit, for apart from Me you can do nothing. 6 If anyone does not abide in Me, he is thrown away as a branch and dries up; and they gather them, and cast them into the fire and they are burned. 7 If you abide in Me, and My words abide in you, ask whatever you wish, and it will be done for you. 8 My Father is glorified by this, that you bear much fruit, and so prove to be My disciples."—NASB

Jesus directly connected hearing and *doing* . . . which necessitates a physical body.

Jesus said that He only did what He received from the Father. Accordingly, He tells us to hear *and then do* His will.

> **Matthew 7:24-27** [Jesus speaking] "Therefore everyone who hears these words of mine and puts them into practice is like a wise man who built his house on the rock. 25 The rain came down, the streams rose, and the winds blew and beat against that house; yet it did not fall, because it had its foundation on the rock. 26 But everyone who hears these words of mine and does not put them into practice is like a foolish man who built his house on sand. 27 The rain came down, the streams rose, and the winds blew and beat against that house, and it fell with a great crash."

> **My note**: There are no verses before or after Jesus' words here that indicate the fallen house will be rebuilt. I'm not saying it's not possible for God to raise it up . . . it's just not information we are offered.

As noted in the last chapter, Jesus told a parable in Matthew 20 about a man who went to the marketplace early one morning and hired people to work in his vineyard. The same man goes into the marketplace at nine, noon, three, and lastly at five in the evening; each time he finds more people to work in his vineyard. At the end of the day, they each got the same wages. Those who'd worked all day were angry that those who worked the last hour of the day got the same amount of pay.

> **Matthew 20:9-12** [Jesus speaking] "The workers who were hired about five in the afternoon came and each received a denarius. 10 So when those came who were hired first, they expected to receive more. But each one of them also received a denarius. 11 When they received it, they began to grumble against the landowner. 12 'These who were hired last worked only one hour,' they said, 'and you have made them equal to us who have borne the burden of the work and the heat of the day.'

Jesus said the Kingdom of heaven was "like this." The greater context of Jesus' words is a discourse on sharing, willingness to share, and following God with all our hearts, without comparison to others. All of these, including the parable above involve *physical presence*. Even the ones who came in at the end of the day **accepted the offer** and worked.

Jesus' words shouldn't be disconnected from His actions. I invite those who believe that Jesus "drags" all people to salvation to find Him doing that in any book of the Bible. He lived a life of sacrificial giving (not taking). During His walk here on earth, He rejected those who rejected Him, accepted all who humbled themselves and believed. I see no exceptions to this.

THE CONTEXT OF JESUS' WORDS: LAYING DOWN HIS LIFE

John 10:11 [Jesus speaking] "I am the Good Shepherd. The Good Shepherd risks and lays down His [own] life for the sheep." [AB]

John 10:15 [Jesus speaking] "This is why the Father loves me: because I freely lay down my life. And so I am free to take it up again. No one takes it from me. I lay it down of my own free will. I have the right to lay it down; I also have the right to take it up again."

John 10:17 [Jesus speaking] "The reason my Father loves me is that I lay down my life—only to take it up again."

John 10:18 [Jesus speaking] "No one can take my life from me. I sacrifice it voluntarily. For I have the authority to lay it down when I want to and also to take it up again. For this is what my Father has commanded."

The Greek word translated "life" in these passages is *yuch* [lxxii] *(*which lexicons also spell *psuche*). It is pronounced psoo-*khay'* and I'm told that it's where we get our word "psyche." [lxxiii] *Yuch* was considered the place of our sentience—the seat of personhood and possibly the place where we reflect God's image.

Thayer's and Smith's Bible Dictionary says,

the soul

A. the seat of the feelings, desires, affections, aversions (our heart, soul etc.)

B. the (human) soul in so far as it is constituted that by the right use of the aids offered it by God it can attain its highest end and secure eternal blessedness, the soul regarded as a moral being designed for everlasting life

C. the soul as an essence which differs from the body and is not dissolved by death (distinguished from other parts of the body) "the seat of the feelings, desires, affections, aversions (our heart, soul etc.) [lxxiv]

---

lxxii "life" #5590, Strong's Exhaustive Concordance of the Bible, ©1800 by James Strong, Public Domain

lxxiii "Psuche" *Thayer and Smith, The New Testament Greek Lexicon*" <http://www.studylight.org/lex/grk/view.cgi?number=5590>. The New Testament Greek Lexicon based on Thayer's and Smith's Bible Dictionary plus others; this is keyed to the large Kittel and the "Theological Dictionary of the New Testament." These files are public domain

lxxiv Ibid.

Jesus commanded those who would follow Him (to become His disciples) to also take up their crosses (to be willing to lose *their* lives).

> **Matthew 16:24-27** Then Jesus said to his disciples, "Whoever wants to be my disciple must deny themselves and take up their cross and follow me. 25 For whoever wants to save their *life* will lose it, but whoever loses their *life* for me will find it. 26 What good will it be for someone to gain the whole world, yet forfeit their *soul*? Or what can anyone give in exchange for their *soul*? 27 For the Son of Man is going to come in his Father's glory with his angels, and then he will reward each person according to what they have done. (All words in italics are "*yuch*").

Who are Jesus' disciples?

> **Matthew 7:21** "Not everyone who says to Me, 'Lord, Lord,' will enter the kingdom of heaven, but he who does the will of My Father who is in heaven will enter."—NASB

> **Matthew 10:38** Whoever does not take up their cross and follow me is not worthy of me.

> **Matthew 16:24** Then Jesus said to his disciples, "Whoever wants to be my disciple must deny themselves and take up their cross and follow me."

> **Mark 8:34** Then he called the crowd to him along with his disciples and said: "Whoever wants to be my disciple must deny themselves and take up their cross and follow me."

> **Luke 9:13** Then he said to them all: "Whoever wants to be my disciple must deny themselves and take up their cross daily and follow me."

> **Luke 13:23-27** And someone said to Him, "Lord, are there just a few who are being saved?" And He said to them, 24 "Strive to enter through the narrow door; for many, I tell you, will seek to enter and will not be able. 25 Once the head of the house gets up and shuts the door, and you begin to stand outside and knock on the door, saying, ' Lord, open up to us!' then He will answer and say to you, 'I do not know where you are from.' 26 Then you will begin to say, 'We ate and drank in Your presence, and You taught in our streets'; 27 and He will say, 'I tell you, I do not know where you are from; depart from Me, all you evildoers.'"—NASB

> **Luke 14:27** "And whoever does not carry their cross and follow me <u>cannot be my disciple.</u>"

> **Luke 14:33** In the same way, those of you who do not give up everything you have cannot be my disciples.

> **John 8:31** To the Jews who had believed him, Jesus said, "If you hold to my teaching, you are really my disciples."

> **John 13:35** "By this everyone will know that you are my disciples, if you love one another."

> **John 15:8** "This is to my Father's glory, that you bear much fruit, showing yourselves to be my disciples."

> **John 18:37** Therefore Pilate said to Him, "So You are a king?" Jesus answered," You say correctly that I am a king. For this I have been born, and for this I have come into the world, to testify to the truth. Everyone who is of the truth hears My voice."—NASB

> **James 1:12** Blessed is the one who perseveres under trial because, having stood the test, that person will receive the crown of life that the Lord has promised to those who love him.

Hebrews 10:39 But we do not belong to those who shrink back and are destroyed, but to those who have faith and are saved.

2 Timothy 2:10-13 Therefore I endure everything for the sake of the elect, that they too may obtain the salvation that is in Christ Jesus, with eternal glory. Here is a trustworthy saying: If we died with him, we will also live with him; if we endure, we will also reign with him. If we disown him, he will also disown us; if we are faithless, he remains faithful, for he cannot disown himself.

Titus 1:16 They claim to know God, but by their actions they deny him. They are detestable, disobedient and unfit for doing anything good.

NOTE: The words, *take up, carry, give up, does ,do, endure, persevere, bear fruit, actions,* and *hear* all speak of physical presence—as in while we have existence here on earth.

What did Jesus *command* His disciples to do?

Matthew 28:18-20 Then Jesus came to them and said, "All authority in heaven and on earth has been given to me. 19 Therefore go and *make disciples of all nations*, baptizing them in the name of the Father and of the Son and of the Holy Spirit, 20 and teaching them to obey everything I have commanded you. And surely I am with you always, to the very end of the age."

I don't think Jesus was asking the disciples to merely *evangelize* the nations (as in pressing for an emotional commitment at an altar or a one-time prayer). He was asking them to lose their own lives in LIVING OUT the gospel, showing the way to the Father through Jesus. Is He asking anything different of us?

God Doesn't Have a Witness Protection Program

I'm not saying He doesn't watch over every single one of us . . . but truly being His witness can and will eventually cost you. Jesus said so.

The problem is that so much of what parades around calling itself "Christianity" is an empty show—words and no life. Many Christians are taught to go out with a formula for converting people (to "make the deal") . . . without much regard to what it means, what should happen next, or what kind of lives they themselves model in front of their families, neighbors, and coworkers. Jesus called us to make disciples, not give sales pitches for a one-time prayer.

Discipleship requires conscious choices coupled with living them out (physical presence).

Gnosticism was the belief that only the "spiritual" was good, that anything connected to the flesh was evil.

A definition of the spirit of the antichrist at work is the separating of (or divorcing) the word "Christ" from the word "Jesus" in such a way that the word "Christ" is solely a spirit that can be employed apart from Jesus (a "christ spirit"). When New Testament Scriptures refer to "Christ," they are referring to Jesus the man.

1 John 4:1-3 Dear friends, do not believe every spirit, but test the spirits to see whether they are from God, because many false prophets have gone out into the world. 2 This is how you can recognize the Spirit of God: Every spirit that acknowledges that Jesus Christ has come in the flesh is from God, 3 but every spirit that does not acknowledge Jesus is not from God. This is the spirit of the antichrist, which you have heard is coming and even now is already in the world.

Jesus came IN THE FLESH (in order to save those of us who inhabit flesh). There is no evidence that declares He came to save Satan, demons, or that He saves people after they're dead.

The judgments at the white throne involve *doing* or *lack of doing*. All this means those who don't know Jesus (or falsely claim to know Him), will be judged by what they do in this physical realm.

Revelation 21:8 "But the cowardly, the unbelieving, the vile, the murderers, the sexually immoral, those who practice magic arts, the idolaters and all liars—they will be consigned to the fiery lake of burning sulfur. This is the second death."

CHAPTER 11—Christian history and concepts of the past

Apokatastasis

What if some in the early church really DID believe in Universalism or Universal Reconciliation? Rob Bell says that at the "center" of traditions in Christianity and since the "first church" there have been people who believed that "hell is not forever . . . and all will be reconciled to God." [lxxv]

The Christian Universalist Association states the cornerstone of their belief is that Hell isn't eternal because, "God has planned the universe to produce a positive outcome for all sentient beings He has ever created." They also believe that in the early church this idea was called "*apokatastasis*" which they define as "the reconciliation of all things." The CUA also claims that this was "recognized as an important teaching of the Gospel during the first few centuries of Christianity."[lxxvi]

Despite the fact that the word is only used ONCE in the New Testament and the context around the word doesn't support the Universalist's definition of it, again and again I see the word "*apokatastasis*" used as a support beam for Universalism. They claim that their concept of the word was a "recognized" and "important teaching" of the "first few centuries of Christianity," or in the "first Church."

I question their use of the term "*first.*"

By definition, "first" would have to include the *first century* of the Church, the *first* leaders of the Church, the *first* gatherings of believers—and since I don't believe there is any evidence that the *first Church* or people in the *first century* of the Church gave the Universalist version of "*apokatastasis*" serious consideration (much less a place of importance or centrality)—I would suggest that, in the interest of honesty, Universalists quit using the term "first" in reference to the Church and their belief.

WHAT IF, however, there are *some* ancient writings—if not in the "first" church—in the *early* Church, (say in the third and fourth centuries) that *support* the Universalistic concept of "*apokatastasis*"?

Indeed, such writings *do* exist and, yes, some of them are written by people who considered themselves to be Christians and were teachers. But even within the time where these writings originated (Third Century), I think you would be hard pressed to say *apokatastasis* was "recognized" as an "important" doctrine by the majority in the early Church.

---

lxxv Rob Bell Rob Bell, *Love Wins, A Book About Heaven, Hell, and the Fate of Every Person Who Ever Lived*, (New York HarperCollins Publishers 2011) 91-92

lxxvi From the *Universal Salvation* page of the Christian Universalist Assoc. website at http://www.christianuniversalist.org/articles/universalsalvation.html (16 Feb. 2012)

Also, keep in mind the fact that you can find writings that support the idea of a flat earth or the writings of "prominent scientists" (who claimed to be Christians) in the past who stated that the sun revolved around the earth. It doesn't make these ideas true, it just means people had those ideas.

If you look it up on the internet or at the library, you will find an extensive amount of material linking Origen of Alexandria (185-254 A.D.) and possibly his tutor, Clement of Alexandria (150-215 A.D.) to the development of the Universalist's concept of *apokatastasis* and the Universalists' claim that the idea was "in the early Church." (Most commonly, Origen is credited with promotion of the Universalistic idea of *apokatastasis* in the early church.) Much of the material and research concerning this is on Roman Catholic sites and of note are the works of Edward Moore. [lxxvii]

WHAT IF . . . Rather than being a Christian concept, Origen's use of *apokastasis* reflected an ancient (non-Christian) belief?

If you look, you will see that both the term *apokatastasis* and the concepts which Universalists associate with it not only predate Clement and Origen, they actually *predate Christianity*!

Origen was an "ascetic"—which meant he held near and dear many of the same ideas as the stoic philosophers, including *apokatastasis*—the idea of a sort of cosmic recycling with "destruction and rebirth" in a cosmic fire, where "Universal reason" dries up everything—"absorbing and containing all unique expressions." (If you're a *Star Trek®* fan, it's kinda like *the Borg*.) Contained within the stoic idea of *apokatastasis* was the belief that there was "no choice" for humanity—all of whom were under the great force of *destiny*. They believed that the way to a virtuous life was to accept "one's allotted station in life." [lxxviii]

QUESTIONS: Isn't it interesting that so many pagan societies had this same concept and used it to keep the powerful in power (such as in the Caste system in India in ages past)? Is this why so many Christian Universalists see no need to share the Gospel? Is this why some feel motivated to simply help people become *better* at staying where they are at?

If you look at the life of Origen as chronicled on Wikipedia [lxxix] and other sites, you'll see he had all manner of odd (and some scary) beliefs which would be openly rejected now, but in reading his works, you can see in some of it the fatalistic thread that runs through Roman Catholicism and Universalism.

> The Bible declares that abiding in Christ isn't merely reformative—it's *transformational*. In Christ your heart and mind aren't re-formed but made *new*. And, unlike Universalists and the philosophers who inspired them, I believe you have a choice in what you believe. Choose well! ☺

---

lxxvii Notes on the *Development of a Noble Notion* by Edward Moore at http://www.romancatholicism.org/origen-apokatastasis.htm and the site Quodlibet Online Journal at http://www.quodlibet.net/about/terms.shtml

lxxviii Notes on the *Development of a Noble Notion* by Edward Moore at http://www.romancatholicism.org/origen-apokatastasis.htm and the site Quodlibet Online Journal at http://www.quodlibet.net/about/terms.shtml

lxxix http://en.wikipedia.org/wiki/Origen#The_Logos_doctrine_and_cosmology, (May 25, 2012)

CHAPTER 12—Scriptures on topics *other than* Hell that don't work with Universalism

The entirety of Scripture points to God and His means of salvation. I am not the one who decides who goes where . . . but there *is* a dividing process that has been determined by God.

WHO IS YOUR DADDY? Son or Slave

Matthew 12:49 [Jesus] Pointing to his <u>disciples</u>, he said, "Here are my mother and my brothers.

John 8:31-47 . . . Jesus said, "If you hold to my teaching, you are really my disciples. 32 Then you will know the truth, and the truth will set you free."

33 They answered him, "We are Abraham's descendants and have never been slaves of anyone. How can you say that we shall be set free?"

34 Jesus replied, "Very truly I tell you, everyone who sins is a slave to sin. 35 <u>Now a slave has no permanent place in the family</u>, but a son belongs to it forever. 36 So if the Son sets you free, you will be free indeed. 37 I know that you are Abraham's descendants. Yet you are looking for a way to kill me, because you have no room for my word. 38 I am telling you what I have seen in the Father's presence, and you are doing what you have heard from your father."

39 "Abraham is our father," they answered.

"If you were Abraham's children," said Jesus, "then you would do what Abraham did. 40 As it is, you are looking for a way to kill me, a man who has told you the truth that I heard from God. Abraham did not do such things. 41 You are doing the works of your own father."

"We are not illegitimate children," they protested. "The only Father we have is God himself."

42 Jesus said to them, "<u>If God were your Father, you would love me</u>, for I have come here from God. I have not come on my own; God sent me. 43 Why is my language not clear to you? Because you are unable to hear what I say. 44 <u>You belong to your father, the devil, and you want to carry out your father's desires</u>. He was a murderer from the beginning, not holding to the truth, for there is no truth in him. When he lies, he speaks his native language, for he is a liar and the father of lies. 45 Yet because I tell the truth, you do not believe me! 46 Can any of you prove me guilty of sin? If I am telling the truth, why don't you believe me? 47 Whoever belongs to God hears what God says. <u>The reason you do not hear is that **you do not belong to God**</u>."

Matthew 23:15 [Jesus speaking] "Woe to you, teachers of the law and Pharisees, you hypocrites! You travel over land and sea to win a single convert, and when you have succeeded, you make them twice as much a child of hell as you are."

2 Corinthians 6:16b . . .18 For we are the temple of the living God. As God has said. . . . "I will be a Father to you, and you will be my sons and daughters, says the Lord Almighty."
    (Paul is quoting from 2 Samuel 7:8; 7:14)

1 John 3:2 Dear friends, now we are children of God, and what we will be has not yet been made known. But we know that when Christ appears, we shall be like him, for we shall see him as he is.

Contained within all of the above scriptures is the concept that there ARE sons and daughters—and there are also those who are not.

Discipline (or chastisement) is for sons and daughters

Hebrews 12:7-9 As you endure this divine discipline, remember that God is treating you as his own children. Who ever heard of a child who is never disciplined by its father? 8 If God doesn't discipline you as he does all of his children, it means that you are illegitimate and are not really his children at all. 9 Since we respected our earthly fathers who disciplined us, shouldn't we submit even more to the discipline of the Father of our spirits, and live forever? —NLT

Please note that this is applied to discipline *here* and *now* as opposed to the afterlife.

Inheritance is for sons and daughters

Romans 8:9-17 But you are not living the life of the flesh, you are living the life of the Spirit, if the [Holy] Spirit of God [really] dwells within you [directs and controls you]. But if anyone does not possess the [Holy] Spirit of Christ, he is none of His [he does not belong to Christ, is not truly a child of God].

10 But if Christ lives in you, [then although] your [natural] body is dead by reason of sin and guilt, the spirit is alive because of [the] righteousness [that He imputes to you].

11 And if the Spirit of Him Who raised up Jesus from the dead dwells in you, [then] He Who raised up Christ Jesus from the dead will also restore to life your mortal (short-lived, perishable) bodies through His Spirit Who dwells in you.

12 So then, brethren, we are debtors, but not to the flesh [we are not obligated to our carnal nature], to live [a life ruled by the standards set up by the dictates] of the flesh.

13 For if you live according to [the dictates of] the flesh, you will surely die. But if through the power of the [Holy] Spirit you are [habitually] putting to death (making extinct, deadening) the [evil] deeds prompted by the body, you shall [really and genuinely] live forever.

14 For all who are led by the Spirit of God are sons of God.

15 For [the Spirit which] you have now received [is] not a spirit of slavery to put you once more in bondage to fear, but you have received the Spirit of adoption [the Spirit producing sonship] in [the bliss of] which we cry, Abba (Father)! Father!

16 The Spirit Himself [thus] testifies together with our own spirit, [assuring us] that we are children of God.

17 And if we are [His] children, then we are [His] heirs also: heirs of God and fellow heirs with Christ [sharing His inheritance with Him]; only we must share His suffering if we are to share His glory.—Amplified Bible

THE HOLY SPIRIT

The "What We Believe" statement on the Christian Universalist Association website says they believe the Holy Spirit has inspired great texts containing spiritual and moral wisdom "in a variety of cultures and traditions" and that by meditating to connect to "the Spirit within" we will gain understanding of truth.[lxxx]

While I do believe that the Holy Spirit continually moves across the world looking for those whose hearts are searching for God, the Christian Universalist Association website gives the *impression* that those in leadership within the CUA believe all paths lead to God. They also state that the greater understanding of "truths" that we glean from diverse religious beliefs could be applied for the "betterment" of ourselves and the world.

> **1 Corinthians 1:18-21** For the word of the cross is foolishness to those who are perishing, but to us who are being saved it is the power of God. 19 For it is written,
>
> "I will destroy the wisdom of the wise, And the cleverness of the clever I will set aside."
>
> 20 Where is the wise man? Where is the scribe? Where is the debater of this age? Has not God made foolish the wisdom of the world? 21 For since in the wisdom of God the world through its wisdom did not come to know God, God was well-pleased through the foolishness of the message preached to save those who believe.—NASB

Knowledge, meditation, moral teachings, and truths don't save people—Jesus Christ does.

Is the Holy Spirit "within" everyone?

The Christian Universalist Association says ALL people have the "Divine Spirit" within them, that they are all the "powerful offspring of God." [lxxxi]

The Bible *does* say that the Holy Spirit (also called the Spirit of the Lord, the Spirit of God and the Spirit of Christ) can guide or move upon anyone. However, Scripture differentiates between this and the Holy Spirit "dwelling within" everyone. Let's look at what the Bible says about the Holy Spirit.

The ministry of the Holy Spirit is a *necessary* component of salvation.

> **John 3:5-6** Jesus answered, "Very truly I tell you, no one can enter the kingdom of God unless they are born of water *and the Spirit*. Flesh gives birth to flesh, but *the Spirit gives birth to spirit*."
>
> **John 4:23-24** [Jesus speaking] "Yet a time is coming and has now come when the true *worshipers will worship the Father in the Spirit* and in truth, for they are the kind of worshipers the Father seeks. God is spirit, and his worshipers must worship in the Spirit and in truth."
>
> **Romans 8:13-16** For if you live according to [the dictates of] the flesh, you will surely die. But if through the power of the [Holy] Spirit you are [habitually] putting to death (making extinct, deadening) the [evil] deeds prompted by the body, you shall [really and genuinely] live forever. 14 For all who are led by the Spirit of God are sons of God. 15 For [the Spirit

---

lxxx Christian Universalist Association, *What We Believe*, http://christianuniversalist.org/beliefs.html (02/17/2012)

lxxxi Christian Universalist Assoc., *Divine Revelation and Pursuit of the Truth* (linked from the *What We Believe* page) http://www.christianuniversalist.org/articles/revelation-truth.html (02/17/2012)

which] you have now received [is] not a spirit of slavery to put you once more in bondage to fear, but you have received the Spirit of adoption [the Spirit producing sonship] in [the bliss of] which we cry, Abba (Father)! Father! 16 The Spirit Himself [thus] testifies together with our own spirit, [assuring us] that we are children of God.—Amplified Version

The indwelling of the Holy Spirit is promised/given to those who believe the Gospel message and this *always* connected to *faith* in Father God through Jesus Christ:

[***Please note:*** This is not an argument about tongues or gifts of the spirit, just a statement that Scripture says the Holy Spirit is given (as on the day of Pentecost and throughout the book of Acts) when people come to faith in Jesus Christ.]

Acts 2:36-39 "So let everyone in Israel know for certain that God has made this Jesus, whom you crucified, to be both Lord and Messiah!" Peter's words pierced their hearts, and they said to him and to the other apostles, "Brothers, what should we do?" Peter replied, "Each of you must repent of your sins and turn to God, and be baptized in the name of Jesus Christ for the forgiveness of your sins. **Then** you will receive the gift of the Holy Spirit. This promise is to you, and to your children, and even to the Gentiles—all who have been called by the Lord our God." [from the New Living Translation, underline and bold added by me]

Acts 5:32 [Peter and the other apostles replied . . .] "We are witnesses of these things, and so is the Holy Spirit, whom God has given to those who obey him."

Acts 15:7-9 After much discussion, Peter got up and addressed them: "Brothers, you know that some time ago God made a choice among you that the Gentiles might hear from my lips the message of the gospel and believe. God, who knows the heart, showed that he accepted them by giving the Holy Spirit to them, just as he did to us. 9 He did not discriminate between us and them, for he purified their hearts by **faith.**"

Romans 8:8-11 Those who are in the realm of the flesh cannot please God. 9 You, however, are not in the realm of the flesh but are in the realm of the Spirit, if indeed the Spirit of God lives in you. And if anyone does not have the Spirit of Christ, they do not belong to Christ. 10 But if Christ is in you, then even though your body is subject to death because of sin, the Spirit gives life because of righteousness. 11 And if the Spirit of him who raised Jesus from the dead is living in you, he who raised Christ from the dead will also give life to your mortal bodies because of his Spirit who lives in you.

1 Corinthians 2:10-14 . . .The Spirit searches all things, even the deep things of God. 11 For who knows a person's thoughts except their own spirit within them? In the same way no one knows the thoughts of God except the Spirit of God. 12 What we have received is not the spirit of the world, but the Spirit who is from God, so that we may understand what God has freely given us. 13 This is what we speak, not in words taught us by human wisdom but in words taught by the Spirit, explaining spiritual realities with Spirit-taught words. 14 The person without the Spirit does not accept the things that come from the Spirit of God but considers them foolishness, and cannot understand them because they are discerned only through the Spirit.

The infilling or baptism of the Holy Spirit is *always* connected with testimony or service to God.

Acts 1:8 [Jesus speaking] "But you will receive power when the Holy Spirit comes on you; and you will be my witnesses in Jerusalem, and in all Judea and Samaria, and to the ends of the earth."

Acts 5:32 "We are witnesses of these things, and so is the Holy Spirit, whom God has given to those who obey him."

Revelation 19:10 At this I fell at his feet to worship him. But he said to me, "Don't do that! I am a fellow servant with you and with *your brothers and sisters who hold to the testimony of Jesus*. Worship God! For it is the Spirit of prophecy who bears testimony to Jesus."

The indwelling of the Holy Spirit is God's guarantee/seal of eternal life

John 14:16-17 [Jesus speaking] "And I will ask the Father, and he will give you another Advocate, who will never leave you. He is the Holy Spirit, who leads into all truth. **The world cannot receive him, because it isn't looking for him and doesn't recognize him. But you know him, because he lives with you now and later will be in you.**"

Acts 2: 37-39 When the people heard this, they were cut to the heart and said to Peter and the other apostles, "Brothers, what shall we do?" 38 Peter replied, "Repent and be baptized, every one of you, in the name of Jesus Christ for the forgiveness of your sins. And you will receive the gift of the Holy Spirit. 39 The promise is for you and your children and for all who are far off —for all whom the Lord our God will call."

Ephesians 1:13-14 And you also were included in Christ when you heard the message of truth, the gospel of your salvation. ***When you believed*, you were marked in him with a seal, the promised Holy Spirit,** 14 who is a deposit guaranteeing our inheritance until the redemption of those who are God's possession—to the praise of his glory.

Scripture declares that those who are carnal (unspiritual) <u>cannot</u> receive the Holy Spirit

John 14:16-17 [Jesus speaking to His disciples] 16 And I will ask the Father, and he will give you another Advocate, who will never leave you. 17 He is the Holy Spirit, who leads into all truth. <u>The world cannot receive him</u>, because it isn't looking for him and doesn't recognize him. But you know him, because he lives with you now and later will be in you.—NLT

Romans 8:8-11 <u>Those who are in the realm of the flesh cannot please God. 9 You, however, are not in the realm of the flesh but are in the realm of the Spirit, *if* indeed the Spirit of God lives in you. And *if* anyone does not have the Spirit of Christ, they do not belong to Christ. 10 But *if* Christ is in you,</u> then even though your body is subject to death because of sin, the Spirit gives life because of righteousness. 11 And *if* the Spirit of him who raised Jesus from the dead is living in you, he who raised Christ from the dead will also give life to your mortal bodies because of his Spirit who lives in you.

1 Corinthians 2:10-14 "10 . . .The Spirit searches all things, even the deep things of God. 11 For who knows a person's thoughts except their own spirit within them? In the same way no one knows the thoughts of God except the Spirit of God. 12 What we have received is not the spirit of the world, but the Spirit who is from God, so that we may understand what God has freely given us. 13 This is what we speak, not in words taught us by human wisdom but in words taught by the Spirit, explaining spiritual realities with Spirit-taught words. 14 <u>The person without the Spirit does not accept the things that come from the Spirit of God but considers them foolishness, and cannot understand them because they are discerned only through the Spirit.</u>"

Jude 1:18-19 . . . at the last time there will be mockers according to their lusts, leading ungodly lives. These are those setting themselves apart, animal-like ones, not having the Spirit.

THE CHURCH IS THE BODY OF CHRIST. The Head (Jesus) is connected to the Body, not to the world

1 Corinthians 12:12-20 Just as a body, though one, has many parts, but all its many parts form one body, so it is with Christ. 13 For we were all baptized by one Spirit so as to form one body—whether Jews or Gentiles, slave or free —and we were all given the one Spirit to drink. 14 Even so the body is not made up of one part but of many.

15 Now if the foot should say, "Because I am not a hand, I do not belong to the body," it would not for that reason stop being part of the body. 16 And if the ear should say, "Because I am not an eye, I do not belong to the body," it would not for that reason stop being part of the body. 17 If the whole body were an eye, where would the sense of hearing be? If the whole body were an ear, where would the sense of smell be? 18 But in fact God has placed the parts in the body, every one of them, just as he wanted them to be. 19 If they were all one part, where would the body be? 20 **As it is, there are many parts, but one body.**

Colossians 1:18 [Paul speaking of Jesus] And he is the head of the body, the church; he is the beginning and the firstborn from among the dead, so that in everything he might have the supremacy.

Colossians 2:18-20 Do not let anyone who delights in false humility and the worship of angels *disqualify* you. Such a person also goes into great detail about what they have seen; they are puffed up with idle notions by their unspiritual mind. 19 *They have lost connection with the head*, from whom the whole body, supported and held together by its ligaments and sinews, grows as God causes it to grow.

Galatians 5:4 If you seek to be justified and declared righteous and to be given a right standing with God through the Law, you are brought to nothing and so *separated (severed) from Christ.* You have fallen away from grace (from God's gracious favor and unmerited blessing). —Amplified Bible

Ephesians 4:15 Instead, speaking the truth in love, we will grow to become in every respect the mature body of him who is the head, that is, Christ.

Our connection with Jesus mirrors our connection with the Body

1 John 1:7 But if we walk in the light, as he is in the light, we have fellowship with one another, and the blood of Jesus, his Son, purifies us from all sin.—NASB

LIGHT AND DARKNESS

1 John 1:6-7 If we claim to have fellowship with him and yet walk in the darkness, we lie and do not live out the truth. 7 But if we walk in the light, as he is in the light, we have fellowship with one another, and the blood of Jesus, his Son, purifies us from all sin.

2 Corinthians 6:14-16a Do not be yoked together with unbelievers. For what do righteousness and wickedness have in common? Or what fellowship can light have with darkness? 15 What harmony is there between Christ and Belial? Or what does a believer have in common with an unbeliever? 16 What agreement is there between the temple of God and idols? For we are the temple of the living God.

INTERCESSION—LOVE STEPPING INTO OUR TIMELINE

Throughout the Bible, we see that God has always looked for someone to "stand in the gap" for others who would be destroyed by virtue of their dark choices. We see it in Abraham going to fight to save his nephew, Lot. We see it in Moses, offering his own life in order to spare sinful Israel. Again in Abigail who stood between David and the destruction of an entire encampment. In reluctant Jonah who preached to a nation about to be destroyed—so that they would repent and live. Most of all we see it in Jesus Christ, offering Himself as ransom for the world. God WANTS us to intercede for our families, our neighbors, our nation, the world. Sometimes that intercession is in prayer, standing before God on someone's behalf. Other times, it's speaking what God has to say, so that the hearer might take it to heart and change course.

SPIRITUAL WARFARE AND DELIVERANCE—defending and freeing the beloved

There is no doubt in my mind that God loves people. Even the ones we think are unlovable. What we often see as appalling character flaws or unfixable damage in others are actually the "natural" byproducts of this dark world system. Jesus asks us to love broken people with His love, and when we do, chains can be broken, slaves set free.

The Kingdom of Light vs. the kingdom of darkness

Jehovah God is the Father of Light

James 1:16-18 So, my very dear friends, don't get thrown off course. Every desirable and beneficial gift comes out of heaven. The gifts are rivers of light cascading down from the Father of Light. There is nothing deceitful in God, nothing two-faced, nothing fickle. He brought us to life using the true Word, showing us off as the crown of all his creatures.—The Message

Jesus is the Light.

Matthew 4:16 "The people who were sitting in darkness saw a great Light, And those who were sitting in the land and shadow of death, Upon them a Light dawned." [quoting Isaiah, referencing Jesus]—NASB

John 1:4-5 In Him was life, and the life was the Light of men. 5 The Light shines in the darkness, and the darkness did not comprehend it.— NASB

John 8:12 Then Jesus again spoke to them, saying, "I am the Light of the world; he who follows Me will not walk in the darkness, but will have the Light of life."—NASB

Those who follow Jesus now have His light

> **Matthew 5:14-15** "You are the light of the world. A city set on a hill cannot be hidden; 15 nor does anyone light a lamp and put it under a basket, but on the lampstand, and it gives light to all who are in the house. 16 Let your light shine before men in such a way that they may see your good works, and glorify your Father who is in heaven."—NASB

> **Colossians 1:12-14** . . . giving thanks to the Father, who has qualified us to share in the inheritance of the saints in Light. For He rescued us from the domain of darkness, and transferred us to the kingdom of His beloved Son, 14 in whom we have redemption, the forgiveness of sins.

There is a separation between the Kingdom of Light and the kingdom of darkness. Those who belong to the Light should not be united with darkness.

> **John 3:10-21** This is the judgment, that the Light has come into the world, and men loved the darkness rather than the Light, for their deeds were evil. 20 For everyone who does evil hates the Light, and does not come to the Light for fear that his deeds will be exposed. 21 But he who practices the truth comes to the Light, so that his deeds may be manifested as having been wrought in God.—NASB

> **2 Corinthians 6:14** Be ye not unequally yoked together with unbelievers: for what fellowship hath righteousness with unrighteousness? <u>And what communion hath light with darkness?</u>—KJV

As a Christian, I *am* called to love others with His love, but that *doesn't* include helping people to be better slaves of darkness.

The power of personal faith in Jesus. Who do <u>you</u> say He is?

Jesus asked Peter, "Who do YOU say I am?" He asked Mary, the sister of Lazarus, "Do you believe this?" You see, it's not so important what someone *else* believes, it's important to have *personal* belief. Being able to repeat the words of your favorite Bible teacher or even the Bible itself is not a show of faith. What's important to GOD is what YOU believe.

Earlier in the book, I shared many Scriptures on knowing Jesus versus denying Jesus. If we know Him here, He will make us known in Heaven. Faith is more than words. What you say *with faith* has power and what you merely repeat is just words.

> **Acts 19:11-16** God gave Paul the power to perform unusual miracles. 12 When handkerchiefs or aprons that had merely touched his skin were placed on sick people, they were healed of their diseases, and evil spirits were expelled.
>
> 13 A group of Jews was traveling from town to town casting out evil spirits. They tried to use the name of the Lord Jesus in their incantation, saying, "I command you in the name of Jesus, whom Paul preaches, to come out!" 14 Seven sons of Sceva, a leading priest, were doing this. 15 But one time when they tried it, the evil spirit replied, "I know Jesus, and I know Paul, but who are you?" 16 Then the man with the evil spirit leaped on them, overpowered them, and attacked them with such violence that they fled from the house, naked and battered.—NLT

Darkness can't fight darkness and have the final victory

The Gospels of Matthew, Mark, and Luke all record incidents where Jesus cast out demons and the religious leaders said it was because Jesus Himself was possessed.

Mark 3:23-37 Jesus called them over and responded with an illustration. "How can Satan cast out Satan?" he asked. 24 "A kingdom divided by civil war will collapse. 25 Similarly, a family splintered by feuding will fall apart. 26 And if Satan is divided and fights against himself, how can he stand? He would never survive. 27 Let me illustrate this further. Who is powerful enough to enter the house of a strong man like Satan and plunder his goods? Only someone even stronger—someone who could tie him up and then plunder his house."—NLT

"Overcomers" and those who are "victorious"

I invite you to go through the book of Revelation and see the precious and wonderful promises God has made to those who overcome. (All of these promises are tied to something to be overcome here in this realm.)

1 John 5:4-5 for everyone born of God overcomes the world. <u>This is the victory that has overcome the world, even our faith. 5 Who is it that overcomes the world? Only the one who believes that Jesus is the Son of God.</u>

Revelation 2:7 [Jesus speaking] "Whoever has ears, let them hear what the Spirit says to the churches. To the one who is victorious, I will give the right to eat from the tree of life, which is in the paradise of God."

Revelation 2:11 [Jesus speaking] "Whoever has ears, let them hear what the Spirit says to the churches. The one who is victorious will not be hurt at all by the second death."

Revelation 2:17 [Jesus speaking] "Whoever has ears, let them hear what the Spirit says to the churches. To the one who is victorious, I will give some of the hidden manna. I will also give that person a white stone with a new name written on it, known only to the one who receives it."

Revelation 3:4-6 [Jesus speaking] "Yet you have a few people in Sardis who have not soiled their clothes. They will walk with me, dressed in white, for they are worthy. 5 The one who is victorious will, like them, be dressed in white. I will never blot out the name of that person from the book of life, but will acknowledge that name before my Father and his angels. 6 Whoever has ears, let them hear what the Spirit says to the churches."

Revelation 3:11-13 [Jesus speaking] "I am coming soon. Hold on to what you have, so that no one will take your crown. 12 The one who is victorious I will make a pillar in the temple of my God. Never again will they leave it. I will write on them the name of my God and the name of the city of my God, the new Jerusalem, which is coming down out of heaven from my God; and I will also write on them my new name. 13 Whoever has ears, let them hear what the Spirit says to the churches."

Revelation 3:21-22 [Jesus speaking] "To the one who is victorious, I will give the right to sit with me on my throne, just as I was victorious and sat down with my Father on his throne. 22 Whoever has ears, let them hear what the Spirit says to the churches."

Revelation 12:11 <u>And they have overcome (conquered) him [Satan] by means of the blood of the Lamb and by the utterance of their testimony</u>, for they did not love and cling to life even when faced with death [holding their lives cheap till they had to die for their witnessing].— Amplified Bible

To testify is to affirm the truth of a matter. Christians are called of God to give testimony to what Jesus Christ has done in us. We are to do this in DEED and word.

AMBASSADORS

As Christians, we are ambassadors of the Kingdom of Heaven. So what's an ambassador? One who is the legal representative of one government living IN the territory of another government. The ambassador doesn't represent his own desires or interests but those of his King (government). The ambassador's home (the consulate) is considered the sovereign territory of the kingdom he represents.

Colorado doesn't have an ambassador in Idaho—because they are both under the same government (the US). To say that you are an ambassador of the Kingdom of God means that you are not a citizen of this world—while living IN it, you are separate from it. You are here to represent God's interests, not your own. It also means there is a standing recognition on the part of your government that the country where you live is *separate* from the Kingdom you represent.

2 Corinthians 5:17-21 Therefore if anyone is in Christ, he is a new creature; the old things passed away; behold, new things have come. 18 Now all these things are from God, who reconciled us to Himself through Christ and gave us the ministry of reconciliation, 19 namely, that God was in Christ reconciling the world to Himself, not counting their trespasses against them, and He has committed to us the word of reconciliation.

20 Therefore, we are ambassadors for Christ, as though God were making an appeal through us; we beg you on behalf of Christ, be reconciled to God. 21 He made Him who knew no sin to be sin on our behalf, so that we might become the righteousness of God in Him.—NASB

Please note that although Christ was "reconciling the world to Himself" WE still are to go out into that world and make an appeal on His behalf. What is that appeal? "We beg you on behalf of Christ, be reconciled to God. He made Him who knew no sin to be sin on our behalf, so that we might become the righteousness of God in Him."

QUESTIONS: Does Paul assume that all people are now right with God? Do his words speak of dragging people to Christ or drawing them?

JUSTICE

The word "justice" is mentioned one hundred forty-five times in the Bible and there are hundreds more scriptures which contain the *concept* of justice. It is an important topic to the Lord. So what IS justice? To uphold what is right without partiality, to discern truth and decide to act accordingly.

One of the criteria God uses for judging nations is to see whether or not justice is found within them. Are the poor and weak who are unable to defend themselves treated with fairness? Are cases decided with impartiality? In God's eyes, those with money and power shouldn't be able to derail justice. Many of you may nod in agreement . . . but doesn't the whole concept of "justice" MEAN that a decision needs to be made between a course of action that is right and one that is wrong? Doesn't it mean that what was wrongfully taken is returned? Doesn't it mean that sometimes one is exonerated and another is penalized? As little as some may like it . . . The Lord says that He *loves* justice, that He is a God of justice, and that He will judge more harshly corrupt (individuals and nations) who pervert justice. He says He will hold those who serve as leaders and teachers to a higher standard.

Psalm 9:16 The LORD is known by his acts of justice; the wicked are ensnared by the work of their hands.

Psalm 11:7 For the LORD is righteous, he loves justice; the upright will see his face.

Psalm 33:4-5 For the word of the LORD is right and true; he is faithful in all he does. The LORD loves righteousness and justice; the earth is full of his unfailing love.

Psalm 50:6 And the heavens proclaim his righteousness, for he is a God of justice.

Psalm 89:14 Righteousness and justice are the foundation of your throne; love and faithfulness go before you.

Psalm 97:2 Clouds and thick darkness surround him; righteousness and justice are the foundation of his throne.

Isaiah 1:16-17 Wash and make yourselves clean. Take your evil deeds out of my sight; stop doing wrong. Learn to do right; seek justice. Defend the oppressed. Take up the cause of the fatherless; plead the case of the widow.

Isaiah 1:27 Zion will be delivered with justice, her penitent ones with righteousness.

Isaiah 9:7 (A PROPHECY ABOUT JESUS)—Of the increase of his government and peace there shall be no end, upon the throne of David, and upon his kingdom, to order it, and to establish it with judgment and with justice from henceforth even forever. The zeal of the LORD of hosts will perform this.

Isaiah 30:15 & 18 For thus said the Lord God, the Holy One of Israel: In returning [to Me] and resting [in Me] you shall be saved; in quietness and in [trusting] confidence shall be your strength. But you would not . . . And therefore the Lord [earnestly] waits [expecting, looking, and longing] to be gracious to you; and therefore He lifts Himself up, that He may have mercy on you and show loving-kindness to you. For the Lord is a God of justice. Blessed (happy, fortunate, to be envied) are all those who [earnestly] wait for Him, who expect and look and long for Him [for His victory, His favor, His love, His peace, His joy, and His matchless, unbroken companionship]!—AMP

Jeremiah 5:27-29 "Like cages full of birds, their houses are full of deceit; they have become rich and powerful 28 and have grown fat and sleek. Their evil deeds have no limit; they do not seek justice. They do not promote the case of the fatherless; they do not defend the just cause of the poor. 29 Should I not punish them for this?" declares the LORD. "Should I not avenge myself on such a nation as this?"

Micah 6:8 He has showed you, O man, what is good. And what does the Lord require of you but to do justly, and to love kindness and mercy, and to humble yourself and walk humbly with your God? [Amplified Bible]

Matthew 5:6 [Jesus speaking] "**God blesses those who hunger and thirst for justice, for they will be satisfied.**"

Matthew 12:18-21 [applying a prophecy to Jesus] "Look at my Servant, whom I have chosen. He is my Beloved, who pleases me. I will put my Spirit upon him, and he will proclaim justice to the nations. 19 He will not fight or shout or raise his voice in public. 20 He will not crush the weakest reed or put out a flickering candle. Finally he will cause justice to be victorious. 21 And his name will be the hope of all the world." [from Isaiah 42:1-4] —NLT

Matthew 23:23 [Jesus speaking] "What sorrow awaits you teachers of religious law and you Pharisees. Hypocrites! For you are careful to tithe even the tiniest income from your herb gardens, but you ignore the more important aspects of the law—justice, mercy, and faith. You should tithe, yes, but do not neglect the more important things."—NLT

Luke 18:1-8 [Jesus speaking] Then Jesus told his disciples a parable to show them that they should always pray and not give up. 2 He said: "In a certain town there was a judge who neither feared God nor cared about men. 3 And there was a widow in that town who kept coming to him with the plea, 'Grant me justice against my adversary.'"

4 "For some time he refused. But finally he said to himself, 'Even though I don't fear God or care about men, 5 yet because this widow keeps bothering me, I will see that she gets justice, so that she won't eventually wear me out with her coming!'"

6 And the Lord said, "Listen to what the unjust judge says. 7 **And will not God bring about justice for his chosen ones, who cry out to him day and night?** Will he keep putting them off? 8 I tell you, he will see that they get justice, and quickly. However, when the Son of Man comes, will he find faith on the earth?"

Acts 17:30-31 [Paul the apostle speaking] "In the past God overlooked such ignorance, but now he commands all people everywhere to repent. For he has set a day when he will judge the world with justice by the man he has appointed. He has given proof of this to everyone by raising him from the dead."

Revelation 6:9-10 When he opened the fifth seal, I saw under the altar the souls of those who had been slain because of the word of God and the testimony they had maintained. They called out in a loud voice, "How long, Sovereign Lord, holy and true, until you judge the inhabitants of the earth and avenge our blood?"

In many ways, I believe that Universalism, is an attempt to take *people* out of "the box" of Church—but the result is that *God, His mercy, and His justice* are placed in a box of man's flawed and limited sense of "fairness" instead.

John 8:14-18 Jesus replied, "You're right that you only have my word. But you can depend on it being true. I know where I've come from and where I go next. You don't know where I'm from or where I'm headed. You decide according to what you can see and touch. I don't make judgments like that. But even if I did, my judgment would be true because I wouldn't make it out of the narrowness of my experience but in the largeness of the One who sent me, the Father. That fulfills the conditions set down in God's Law: that you can count on the testimony of two witnesses. And that is what you have: You have my word and you have the word of the Father who sent me."

WHAT *WAS* IT ABOUT THE PHARISEES THAT GRIEVED AND ANGERED JESUS?

Many of Jesus' harshest words were spoken to the Pharisees and Sadducees—the religious leaders of the day. Even today, the term "Pharisee!" is hurled at people we deem to be religious hypocrites.

Well, let's think about this for a moment. Was Jesus angry at them for keeping the law or telling others to keep it? No. He was angry that those who were claiming to be the **sons of Abraham** who stood in the place of **justice**, those who claimed to have the **Light of God**, who said they had **power over darkness**, who professed the **wisdom from the Holy Spirit** were manipulating the language of God's word to get what they wanted out of it.

Jesus said that the Pharisees were men who "searched the Scriptures daily" thinking they could declare themselves righteous as long as they found some loophole or interpretation of a word that justified what they did. When the Law was insufficient for their purposes, they would cite "tradition" (often rooted in the Pagan beliefs in the people groups around them) as equal to or above the law and continue on their merry way. In today's terminology, they were "workin' it." They created a system which would reward their ways and means—and it was pretty much perfect as far as they were concerned.

But were these men righteous in Jesus' eyes? Did the fact that they could find a clever way to read something *into* the Law or quote it have any sway whatsoever on Jesus? Did the fact that they could absolve one another of their crimes against the poor and helpless make it okay? Did the fact that something was "tradition" have any traction with Jesus? No. They were attempting to "cover" sin with a device of their own making, and in the process they were blocking the way for those who were sincerely seeking God.

ALL of us can find words or verses in Scripture that we can creatively interpret in ways we think will cover our sins. We can place "tradition" on a pedestal and let it overshadow what God says to the contrary. All of us can get caught up in religious power games that ultimately block the way for those who are genuinely seeking God. But in the end, does our ability to do these things make them right? Will God say, "Oh, you got Me *there*! Go figure! In the light of your brilliant interpretation, come on into Heaven!" . . . ?

I don't know about you but I get very concerned when someone takes an obscure sentence or word in the Bible and makes this whole big deal out of it, saying "It HAS to be this way!" If it's so important, why is it so obscure?

I've seen articles written by Universalists that say if God doesn't save *everybody* that He's not God or that He's "cruel" and not worthy of our worship. Yikes!

Just because so many of the teachers of Universal Reconciliation used to stand in pulpits and preach about the fires of Hell doesn't now mean a (self-imposed) penance of saying, "there is no Hell" or, "Hell is temporary" is the right thing to do. A course correction that takes you away from the rocks on one side of the river only to crash you into the rocks on the *other* side of the river isn't a *beneficial* correction for you or those who may be in the boat with you.

Could ALL of us tone down the "it HAS to be this way" rhetoric and look at what God is really trying to impart to us? Could we stop letting tradition and dogma trump Scripture and the voice of the Holy Spirit?

I have no problem with asking God to sort things out. I have no problem with looking at Scripture in different lights, looking at different translations and teachings, allowing them to be weighed and discussed—leaving nothing off the table. What I *do* have a problem with is people "workin' it" to make it say something it doesn't really say. I do have a problem with people taking what someone in the third century espoused and trying to stretch it over the entire Church. I do have a problem with allowing Greek philosophy or pagan beliefs to put on the garb of "tradition" and overshadow the cross of Jesus Christ, HIS call to BE disciples, and to go find more.

CHAPTER 13—Revelations that Changed the course of Christendom

Can Universalism be considered a "revelation" that came from God? Can it be compared to other revelations in Church history that changed the course of Christian thought and practice (such as Luther bringing the doctrine of grace to light or the revelation that slavery was wrong)?

Let's think about that a moment. Certainly, in 1517 when Luther nailed his thesis on the door of the Castle Church in Wittenberg, Germany, it was the beginning of a revolution that eventually rippled through the entirety of the Christian world. Reading his Bible, Luther realized something: We are reconciled to God . . . not by works or ceremonies . . . but by faith, given by the grace of God!

But being reconciled by faith wasn't a *new* concept, it wasn't *invented* by Luther. It wasn't a secret hidden for all time until Luther read it. Faith was key to the gospel preached in the church of the first century. So even though the concept became buried under the doctrines and traditions of churches (who kept the Bible away from the general public)—faith wasn't something "new" that God introduced into the church in the 1500s. Neither was it something God formerly forbade in the Old Testament or the Church but then changed His mind about. It wasn't something that was *vaguely alluded to* in a passage or two of Scripture. Faith was and is a Biblical concept (that was lost for generations when the Bible was hidden from public view).

Slavery. First of all, you need to look at the culture in ancient times to understand what the term really meant at the time. The kind of "slaves" that were permissible by law (in the Old Testament) were what would have been called in later centuries "indentured servants." They were to be servants for a limited amount of time and then were to be set free. Other forms of slavery are recorded in the Bible (yes, even among the nation of Israel), but God found the practice of selling and stealing people an abomination (just as He hated idol worship and corrupted systems of justice). As you look at the accounts of God's people getting off track and absorbing the customs of other people who did such things, remember that these serve as a recorded history of events and actions, not endorsements of what people chose to do.

By the time of the first century Church, slavery (much of it the worst kind) was a way of life in all of the known world. Whole economies depended upon it. But as people's hearts and minds got set free ***in Christ***, they saw the evil of thinking anyone could *own* another human being. Although it happened slowly, the concept of *freedom* in Christ rippled through the entire Church, and changed the way the world saw slavery. It may have seemed a "new" concept, but it was there all the time.

So what about Universalism/Universal Reconciliation? *Has* God said everyone will be in Heaven? Is it an idea we just need to grow into?

Although the concept can be extrapolated out of some verses of Scripture or by using alternate definitions of a few words, the verses which are used to "prove" Universalism are contradicted by a great weight of verses which *do* specifically detail the means by which we are saved. In nearly every case, the verse or word used to "prove" Universalism is *refuted* when read in the context of the very chapter or book of the Bible where it is found.

What if . . .

. . . there are verses which could be understood to be *hinting* at universal salvation? My question is, even if someone believes they can see it there, should the *hint* be allowed to overturn what is openly stated? Should a *shadow* be allowed to replace substance?

Did Jesus ever give a teaching in public and then disown it in private?

If something is essential for us to know, God states and shows it many ways. I don't think the concepts of Universalism/UR meet that standard. While their ideas have *emotional* appeal . . . emotions are feelings, not truth.

CHAPTER 14—Truth and Love . . . Are They the Romeo and Juliet of the Bible?

Jesus Christ came, lived, and died as a humble servant, refusing to use the limitless power at His disposal to take by *force* that which wasn't freely given . . . and yet it is a falsehood to say He had no warnings for people about the condition of their hearts and what they might face after this life if they didn't change. Right now, many outside of Christianity would say the declarations of the Bible against sin are uninformed, intolerant hate-speech. In a seeker sensitive response, some from *inside* the Church are now saying the New Testament has no hard edges, that now it's only about "love."

A while back, there was a commercial on television for an insurance company that made me laugh out loud every time I saw it. The company spokesman says, "Do you think switching to (the insurance company) could save you money on car insurance? Was Abe Lincoln honest?" And then the picture on the screen switches to a (of course pretend) scratchy black and white video of Abe and his wife. She is this chunky little woman trying on a dress with multitudes of folds literally bursting out from under a tightly cinched waistline. Abe is standing behind her and she says, "Does this dress make my backside look big?" The guy who plays Lincoln in this commercial should get an award for his performance. In the seconds after her question, the looks that cross his face as he struggles to find the words to tell her the truth are priceless. Finally, in the lingering silence, she looks back and he meekly gestures as if to say, "Well, maybe a just a little large . . ."

Are genuine truth and genuine love mutually exclusive? Are they *never* to meet and live happily ever after?

People form whole organizations dedicated to defending, promoting, and protesting for the cause of others who are perceived to have been "wronged." But isn't that admitting that some things *are* "wrong?" Vast numbers of our population spend hours every week relishing television reality shows and those depicting surprise interventions and confrontations—where judges, counselors, friends and relatives expose the darkest sides of others in full view of the whole world—and yet many of these same TV viewers think that the God who loves them more than His own life has no right or desire to be honest with them about what's *killing* them?

THE HIGHEST STANDARD: LOVE

Read at weddings, preached in sermons, **1 Corinthians 13, known as the "love chapter" of the Bible, is considered by many to be the gold standard in defining what God's love is.** And, truly, if anyone reads it with an honest heart, it's quite humbling. Few, if any, could ever say they've consistently met this standard in dealing with others. Here is the famous passage in the New Living Translation:

> 1 If I could speak all the languages of earth and of angels, but didn't love others, I would only be a noisy gong or a clanging cymbal. 2 If I had the gift of prophecy, and if I understood all of God's secret plans and possessed all knowledge, and if I had such faith that I could move mountains, but didn't love others, I would be nothing. 3 If I gave everything I have to the poor and even sacrificed my body, I could boast about it; but if I didn't love others, I would have gained nothing.

4 Love is patient and kind. Love is not jealous or boastful or proud 5 or rude. <u>It does not demand its own way.</u> It is not irritable, and it keeps no record of being wronged. 6 It does not rejoice about injustice but <u>rejoices whenever the truth wins out</u>. 7 Love never gives up, never loses faith, is always hopeful, and endures through every circumstance.

8 Prophecy and speaking in unknown languages and special knowledge will become useless. But love will last forever! 9 Now our knowledge is partial and incomplete, and even the gift of prophecy reveals only part of the whole picture! 10 But when the time of perfection comes, these partial things will become useless.

11 When I was a child, I spoke and thought and reasoned as a child. But when I grew up, I put away childish things. 12 Now we see things imperfectly, like puzzling reflections in a mirror, but then we will see everything with perfect clarity. All that I know now is partial and incomplete, but then I will know everything completely, just as God now knows me completely.

13 Three things will last forever—faith, hope, and love—and the greatest of these is love.

GOD'S Love Never Fails

Those who teach Universalism/UR would take verse 8 of this passage (translated "Love never fails" in many English versions) and say that this verse, coupled with verses from elsewhere in the Bible that say "God does what He wills and no one can stop Him," add up to everyone in heaven.

Are they not reading the whole passage of 1 Corinthians 13? What about "it [love] does NOT demand its own way"? Genuine love wants but doesn't force a genuine return of affection.

What about "It [love] does NOT rejoice about injustice but rejoices whenever the TRUTH wins out"?

Does anyone else find it odd that, in the middle of a statement about the highest form of love . . . are words about rejoicing when "TRUTH wins"? But what if, in order for <u>truth</u> to "win out," someone had to experience hurt or abandon a desired pathway right here on earth? Would it be right to ask for such a scenario? Could *love* rejoice in someone's loss? Can it actually be consistent with the Lord's nature [love] to desire such things as truth and justice? Yes. It is a mystery to all of us . . . but only in God are all these things met together.

> **Psalm 85:10** Unfailing love and truth have met together. Righteousness and peace have kissed!—NLT

We are not called to make excuses for God. Neither are we called to encourage the thought that He will comply with our sense of fairness. Because, with God, not just any ol' kind of "loving" will do.

A love that lies or enables is *false* love.

> **Psalm 5:9** My enemies cannot speak a truthful word. Their deepest desire is to destroy others. Their talk is foul, like the stench from an open grave. <u>Their tongues are filled with flattery.</u>—NLT

> **Proverbs 27:6** Faithful are the wounds of a friend; but the kisses of an enemy are deceitful.—KJV

Job 5:18 [speaking of the Lord] "For he wounds, but he also binds up; he injures, but his hands also heal."

1 John 3:18 Dear children, let us not love with words or speech but with actions <u>and in truth</u>.

John 18:3 [Jesus said] "Everyone on the side of truth listens to me."

See, there's no *real* love if there is no room for genuineness or honesty. Love that enables death through flattery or feigned ignorance isn't *real* love! Jesus is the embodiment of love *and* truth, met together in perfection. If you would know Jesus, you must allow yourself to embrace all that He is. Those who are unwilling to know His Truth, don't fully know His Love. Those who only want to dole out the hard cold "facts," won't fully know His Love, either. Truth and Love are met together as one in Him.

The same love that moved Jesus to give up *everything* for you is also the love that will *never lie* to you.

Earlier in the book I spoke of the philanthropic, "golden rule" sort of love that seems to be the ultimate commandment of Universalism and UR. But I ask: Is this what the love of God calls us to?

1 Corinthians 13:3 If I gave everything I have to the poor and even sacrificed my body, I could boast about it; but if I didn't love others, I would have gained nothing.

This verse is comparing *philanthropy* (and/or showy acts of charity) to God's genuine love of others. In God's love there is no falsehood or pretense. It's about loving God first, then letting His love flow through us to others. Without *this* kind of love, Paul says, our philanthropy is meaningless.

No Christian is called to be all truth and no love. By the same token, no Christian is given the mandate *or the right* to dismiss a warning from God in order to keep from offending others. Jesus wants *genuine love*, not love that is coerced OR brought about by presenting a false picture of Him. Jesus isn't in the Conquistador's call to convert now or be slaughtered. He isn't the blond, blue-eyed (non-Jewish) Aryan savior presented by the Nazis in order to keep as many Germans as possible goose-stepping their way toward Hitler in the 1930s. Nor is Jesus the powerless teacher of moral lessons in the Thomas Jefferson Bible (with all the inconvenient truths omitted).

> **Jesus says, "I AM who I AM." To present Him as any less (or other) than who He is, is to do a disservice to Jesus, to yourself, and to the world.**

CHAPTER 15—Making Christianity about Jesus Christ

All of this boils down to what people are willing to place their faith in . . . the One (or the thing) to which they will lead others. Will we place our hope in Jesus Christ or upon wishful thinking? Are we to live by faith in a scenario we've pasted together, or by placing our faith in Jesus? Are we to become disciples of Jesus or followers of a concept? Am I part of the Body, or just a member of a humanitarian organization?

> **As much as our control-freaky hearts would like a one-sided, formulaic God that we can adequately describe and fully understand . . . He is *not* some tame god of our own making . . . and we cannot understand all of His ways.**

The Bible says Jesus is the Truth *and* that He *will* judge with *justice*—but it also says He is the full embodiment of Love. He has presence, intelligence, and feeling BEYOND our capacity to fully comprehend. He isn't a two dimensional, predictable, figure that's been fixed like text on a page, or bits of color on a canvas or stained glass window. We could look at any one aspect of God (such as holiness, prosperity, or love) and say we have found *a* truth, an aspect of God—but as we read the Bible and live our lives in ways that center on *the single aspect* rather than Jesus we could contradict the bigger picture He has given us (and possibly be honoring an idol). Formulas are often made from a slice of "truth" that hasn't been brought into balance with the whole truth of all that Jesus is and does. I believe that such is the case with Universalism/Universal Reconciliation.

Salvation based on <u>faith</u> in the promise of God (embodied in Jesus Christ, God's one and *only* begotten Son) is specifically made in Scripture—in Old and New Testaments, in the Gospels, through the apostles, and in the epistles. The promise is made directly, in context, in metaphors, types, shadows, and seen in the actions of God. This isn't some fragment of truth or an obscure idea that was brought to life by creative interpretation. The qualifying statement of salvation "by faith" (by believing God's promise, trusting Him) is made from Genesis to Revelation. The promise isn't changed or negated by anyone's refusal to accept it. The promise cannot be amended, revoked, or rerouted by mankind—it's *God's* promise.

I believe that salvation is a God-given choice which is offered to all. While I agree that there will be those in Heaven who didn't know the name "Jesus" (such as Abraham whose righteousness was reckoned to him "by faith" in the *promise* of God), I will state emphatically that the only *certainty* of Heaven is through faith in Jesus Christ. Specifically who else might meet the criteria of "being reckoned righteous by faith" is up to the Lord—and Scripture shows repeatedly that He will judge people on a case by case basis.* Unlike the world's court where man presides, God's throne of judgment is not limited in insight, wisdom, knowledge, energy, time, or resources.

*Here are some of the New Testament Scriptures which demonstrate that God views/judges each person individually:

>Matthew 12:30-32, 12:46-50, 25:1-13, 25:14-28, 25:32-46,
>Mark 3:28-29, 3:32-34, 9:42-48, 16:15-16,
>Luke 8:20-21, 9:23-24,
>John 1:12-13, 3:3-18, 5:24-30, 5:28-29, 6:39-40, 8:19-24, 8:49-51, 14:6, 15:5-6, 20:31,
>Acts 2:21, 2:36-39, 10:41-43, 13:38-39, 17:24-31, 26:12-18,
>Romans 3:21-26,
>1 Corinthians 5:9-11, 6:9-10,
>Galatians 5:19-21,
>Colossians 1:21-23
>2 Thessalonians 1:4-9,
>2 Timothy 4:1-8,
>Hebrews 10:39, 11:6,
>James 1:12,
>2 Peter 2:1-3, 2:6-9, 3:3-9,
>1 John 2:23-25,
>Revelation 14:9-11, 20:11-15, 21:1-8

While the people in Universalism and UR have the (I say God-given) right to believe anything they want, I don't believe the idea they offer is based on any direct promise of God within the context of the whole Bible, or upon the whole teachings of Jesus, or upon what He *did* within the context of what He said.

I hear the cry of Universalists against the use of Hell as the center of evangelism . . . and I agree that this is an unwise tactic. I understand that many of those who believe in Universalism and Universal Reconciliation may want to comfort people who are uncertain about loved-ones who have passed away. I hear what they are saying. I am mindful of the kindness Universalists hope to see offered at the Judgment seat—but I also find it a great mystery that some of those who claim to have discovered the ultimate in Love wouldn't make the One who IS love—Jesus Christ—the center of their life and message instead of a concept that contradicts His words and deeds.

Is it so embarrassing to admit we don't have all the answers on eternity that we feel we must fill in all the blanks with wishful thinking? I'll say it right now: I don't have all the answers . . . but I DO know the One who *is* the Answer, and I'm content to trust Him with all the things I can't see, touch, and understand right now.

It really IS about love

Loving God should be at the root of everything that takes place in Christian life. Loving others should be the outflow—the growth and fruit of that root. How many Christians actually LIVE OUT the commands to love God first, and then to love our neighbors? It's very sobering. Indeed, we cannot claim to *be* true disciples of Jesus (much less go and make other disciples) if we don't have the root of loving the Lord first and foremost, with the outflow of the fruit of loving others (with His love).

Love God *first* . . . *then* love your neighbor. And if you truly love them, you will speak the truth in love.

I look at the lack of fruit and bad fruit produced in passively "loving" people along on their path to death, thinking that we need not bother to mention Jesus to a Hindu or an atheist or someone completely lost in addiction because "God made them that way," and "they're saved but they just don't know it yet." I look at the bad fruit that is produced when people are led to believe that they can live like Hell now and apologize later. On the other hand, I look at "Evangelical" Christians who are all talk and no substance—and I am ashamed.

Where are Gandhi, John Lennon, Elvis, and Princess Di right now?

I know, in this information age when data is just a Google search away, when we are bombarded with input, high tech gadgets, and new discoveries it's hard for some people (especially people outside faith in God) to believe that there are things that we can't know. There are people who have convinced themselves that, given sufficient time, science, and equipment, humanity could unravel every mystery. And, if you're one of those people, whether you realize it or not, you've placed your belief (faith) in something—man's abilities—rather than the Lord.

But, for those of us who often say that God is (and can do things) beyond our capacity to fully grasp . . . *can't we allow this to be more than an empty confession?* What is *faith* if there is no trust? For me, as a person who claims to believe in God, to spend hours, days, or years agonizing over the final disposition of Gandhi, or someone in my family, or anybody else who has died is a pointless rabbit trail.

WHAT IF . . . you want to believe that Jesus desires to save every single person? Congratulations. You have heard the heartbeat of Jesus. But there is a difference between *this* and saying that He will drag everyone to Heaven.

Not one of us has been given the task of deciding where any particular person will (or will not) end up, since only God knows the entirety of anyone's life and heart, what they did in secret, what their final thoughts were. I am certain that there are still secrets in Heaven which we do not know. What Jesus has asked us to take on *faith* is that <u>He is both merciful **and** just</u>, that He loves every single one of us—*and His judgments are higher than ours.*

ARE OUR HANDS OPEN OR CLOSED?

Can't we just rest in Him? Should we decide what Jesus MUST do at the judgment seat in order to be worthy of our love? He has withheld *nothing* from us . . . can't we simply rest in Him?

> **Jeremiah 29:11-13** "For I know the plans I have for you," declares the LORD, "plans to prosper you and not to harm you, plans to give you hope and a future. Then you will call on me and come and pray to me, and I will listen to you. You will seek me *and find me when you seek me with all your heart.*"

I will tell you that I myself have lost loved ones and family members. I've lost two children who died in infancy . . . but I am at peace. I've lost friends to suicide. But I am at peace. My own beloved father died just before I completed this book. But I am at peace. That's not to say I feel no sorrow over their deaths or that I haven't keenly missed them here . . . but I am at peace regarding the "outcome" of every one of them. Why is that? Because I have come to know God and felt His grace flowing like a river to me. I have known His love, and I have *faith* that on that final Day I will be satisfied. I will be able, with a full heart, to praise Him as all wise, just, mighty, and merciful. Until then, I have no demands, no must-have scenarios. I want to stand with open hands and simply trust Him. Could I invite you to do the same? Could Christians live simply, loving and *trusting* God first, then loving others with His love, and leave the judgment of who will go where to Him?

I will end this book with a few verses from the book of Romans:

> Scripture reassures us, "No one who trusts God like this—heart and soul—will ever regret it." It's exactly the same no matter what a person's religious background may be: the same God for all of us, acting the same incredibly generous way to everyone who calls out for help. "Everyone who calls, 'Help, God!' gets help."
>
> But how can people call for help if they don't know who to trust? And how can they know who to trust if they haven't heard of the One who can be trusted? And how can they hear if nobody tells them? And how is anyone going to tell them, unless someone is sent to do it? That's why Scripture exclaims,
>
>> A sight to take your breath away!
>> Grand processions of people telling all the good things of God!
>
> But not everybody is ready for this, ready to see and hear and act. Isaiah asked what we all ask at one time or another: "Does anyone care, God? Is anyone listening and believing a word of it?" <u>The point is: Before you trust, you have to listen. But unless Christ's Word is preached, there's nothing to listen to.</u>—Romans 10:11-17, *The Message*

From the publisher:

We hope you have enjoyed this book. If so, would you take a few moments to write an online review on the bookseller's web page?

Reader's Notes:

Reader's Notes:

Other Books from Wild Flower Press, Inc.

You can purchase the *ebook* versions of all our books at Amazon.com, on Smashwords.com, in the Apple iStore, and through many other retail bookseller sites. Many of our books may even be available through your local library (if your library carries ebooks)!

You can also purchase paper versions of our books directly from the Wild Flower Press, Inc. website at: **www.wildflowerpress.biz**, on Amazon.com, CreateSpace, and through many other booksellers. If you order through our website, special pricing is available for orders of 6 or more printed copies being shipped to one address in one order (see our Bulk Sales page for details). We offer secure purchasing through *PayPal®* for people (you need not have a *PayPal®* account to make a purchase).

The Within the Walls trilogy by Stephanie Bennett

Within the Walls, Breaking the Silence, & The Poet's Treasure

This is a fast-paced series with a look into the increasingly digital existence of humanity. As media outlets, corporations, and advertisers seek to mesh simulated life with tangible life, the eventual collision of these two worlds is far from the minds of many who cut their teeth on mommy's IPod® and have never known a time when media wasn't a dominant presence or the driving force in day-to-day existence.

The trilogy brings us to the busy world of the character, Emilya, a creator of virtual vacations in the year 2071. At 29, she hasn't seen much of a need to think about for anything beyond the walls of her highly productive life, but the discovery of a mysterious letter sends her world spinning. Enter the inner chambers of Emilya's search for meaning. Take a careful look within the walls; her story may be closer than you think.

The Scions of the Aegean C series by Terry L. Craig

Scions of the Aegean C, Book 1 is available now

Through the Land of Cloud and Leaf, Book 2 due for release in 2016

The books in this series are in the Steampunk genre. What is Steampunk? It's a subgenre of science fiction and fantasy literature that commonly has several distinct features. Steampunk . . .

- Is often set in an alternative history
- Usually features some aspect of retro-tech—machinery one might have seen in the era of steam engines, and inventions such as H. G. Wells or Jules Verne might have pictured them
- Often depicts at least some portion of society with distinct moral sensibilities
- Shows that society in conflict

The entire series *Scions of the Aegean C*—is in this genre. People leave Earth in the future . . . and end up in an alternate timeline with nothing but what they have onboard their spacecraft and whatever courage or faith they have in their hearts to start life in a new world. A century later, what the descendants of the "Firstlanders" have is retro-technology that only a few people know how to build/use . . . and a divided society that's begging for a shakeup. :-)

The Fellowship of the Mystery trilogy by Terry L. Craig
Gatekeeper, Sojourner, & Swordsman

Inspiring Futuristic Fiction

The trilogy portrays men and women attempting to navigate through a world that is increasingly possessed by the hypocricies of political correctness and relativistic truth.

Apocalyptic Fiction? Yes. About the *timing* of The End? No.
These stories are woven around faith, and are intended to:
- Give both Christians and non-Christians a view of God's grace in the midst of hardship
- Demonstrate ways of living out faith whatever the time
- Shine the light of the Gospel in the darkness

When Jesus spoke of the Last Days . . .

He gave an illustration in a parable about ten virgins . . .
five He dubbed "foolish" . . .
and five He called "wise."

What made the difference? . . .
All were waiting for their bridegroom to return unexpectedly and take them to a prepared place . . . *but* those the Lord deemed "wise," though ready to depart, were also prepared to endure.*

> *Endure: Greek *hupomeno* (hoop-ahm-en-oh) to remain, to tarry behind, to remain i.e. abide, not recede or flee to preserve: under misfortunes and trials to hold fast to one's faith in Christ, to endure, bear bravely and calmly: ill treatments endure. [New Testament Greek Lexicon—King James Version—public domain]

Gatekeeper, Sojourner,* and *Swordsman

Are three ordinary men . . .
> Who by their everyday obedience to Christ, play active roles in the fulfillment of God's will for human history . . .
> Who endure times of great pressure and crisis to produce eternal fruit . . .
> Who—like us all—are unable to know the total significance of their faithful, persistent, obedience.

Together, these three novels demonstrate the fruit of persevering faithfulness and the dangers of being focused on anything other than Jesus Christ. The lives of the people in *Gatekeeper, Sojourner*, and *Swordsman* intersect as increasing pressure refines and defines their characters.

AVAILABLE in SUMMER 2016

A devotional from our newest author, Tonya Brown:
PASSPORT FOR THE JOURNEY, 21 Day Challenge will make a great gift for those preparing to go on mission trips, graduates launching into the next phase of life, or teams embarking on a new endeavor.

The travel-sized devotional will slip easily into any briefcase, purse, or pocket. Each entry in this book can be read in a couple of minutes, but is enough food to meditate on the entire day—great for a personal devotional, or for use by a group as an opener for meetings. The content is written for Millennial Generation believers who are ready to embark on a new experience with God.

Challenging and thought-provoking, PASSPORT FOR THE JOURNEY is divided into three parts each containing seven daily readings. The first section explores God's purposes. The second invites readers into a deeper personal relationship with God. The final segment challenges believers to persevere in their calling.

Wild Flower Press, Inc.

We offer a growing number of free online Bible Studies.

We also offer articles on faith and life from a Christian perspective.

Visit our website at www.wildflowerpress.*biz*